INFLATION FOR REAL ESTATE INVESTORS

THE REAL ESTATE INVESTING
MENTOR
THE AFFORDABLE $50K COACHING ALTERNATIVE

James Orr
The Real Estate Financial Planner™

Published by:

Real Estate Financial Planner LLC
PO Box 2163
Loveland CO 80539

https://RealEstateFinancialPlanner.com

First edition November 2024.
File: 2024-11-06 - Inflation for Real Estate Investors

This publication is designed to provide accurate and authoritative information regarding the subject matter covered. It is sold with the understanding that the publisher is not engaged in rendering legal, accounting or other professional advice or services. If legal advice or other expert advice is required, the services of a competent professional person should be sought.

From a *Declaration of Principles* jointly adopted by a Committee of American Bar Association and a Committee of Publishers and Associations.

This is a work of fiction. References to clients in this book are fictional and have been modified and changed from any possible real situations to protect the identities of clients and to simplify the stories for clarity. In some cases, significant parts of the stories have been changed. In some cases, stories have been completely fabricated to illustrate a concept. Any similarities to people alive or dead is purely coincidental.

AI Disclosure: While James Orr authored the original version of this content, AI was used extensively to draft, proofread, edit, improve and write subsequent versions and variations.

DEDICATION

Dedicated to my wife Tammy. I have no words.

FREE DOWNLOAD

The World's Greatest Real Estate Deal Analysis Spreadsheet™

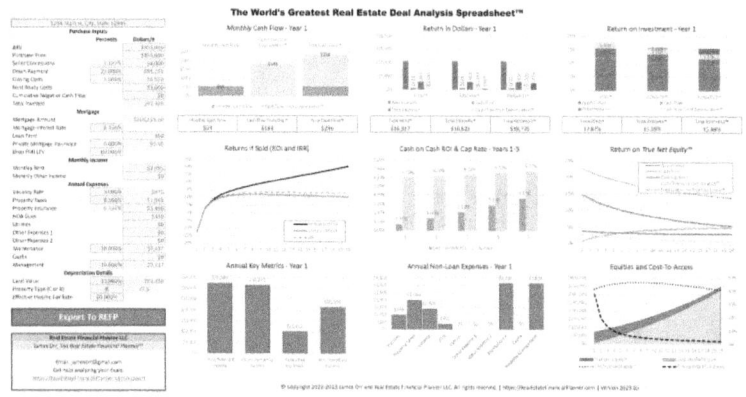

Thank you for purchasing this book and taking the next step toward mastering real estate investing.

As a special bonus, you can download *The World's Greatest Real Estate Deal Analysis Spreadsheet*™ for free. This powerful tool will help you analyze deals like a pro, ensuring you make informed, profitable decisions.

Download your free copy now and start running the numbers with confidence.

https://REFP.com/spreadsheet

Table of Contents

Inflation for Real Estate Investors

I'm writing this the morning after the US presidential election.

It doesn't matter which election because the feelings real estate investors have been associated with any change in leadership: uncertainty about the inflation and the future.

Below I will cover:

- What is inflation (yawn)
- How is inflation measured (double yawn)
- How inflation impacts home ownership versus renters (perking up a bit)
- How inflation impacts real estate investors (you've got my attention)

Specifically, we will look at how a real estate investor in a "historically" normal inflationary environment would achieve financial independence as our baseline.

Then, we will look at how that same strategy would perform in an environment of low inflation. Then, we will look at how that same strategy would perform in a high inflation environment.

How ugly or pretty will it get? And how much impact does this really have?

Along the way, I'll also go off on some inflation-related tangents for real estate investors including asset protection, asset allocation, taxes and 1031 tax deferred exchanges.

Ready? Let's begin.

What Is Inflation?

Inflation is a term you've probably heard thrown around on the news, and as a real estate investor, it's important to understand how it can impact your investments.

At its core, inflation represents the increase in prices of goods and services over time. As prices rise, the purchasing power of your money falls, meaning that the same dollar buys fewer goods and services than before.

In practical terms, think of a loaf of bread that cost $1 but now costs $2. That price increase reflects inflation. The concept applies broadly, from everyday groceries to larger financial commitments, like buying properties or financing real estate deals.

Inflation isn't inherently good or bad—it's simply a reflection of economic forces. For real estate investors, understanding inflation matters because it directly influences your expenses, income, and property values.

When inflation is well-managed, it can even work to your advantage by eroding the "real" value of your debt over time, but when left unchecked, it can lead to significant challenges.

How Is Inflation Measured?

Inflation is measured by tracking the changing prices of a "basket of goods" over time.

This basket represents a variety of products and services that a typical household might purchase, such as food, clothing, healthcare, transportation, and, crucially for real estate investors, housing.

By monitoring how the total cost of this basket shifts, we get a sense of how the cost of living changes, which informs how much more (or less) we need to spend to maintain our standard of living.

In the United States, the primary tool for measuring inflation is the Consumer Price Index (CPI).

The CPI calculates the average change in prices paid by urban consumers for this basket.

Each item is assigned a weight, reflecting its relative importance in an average consumer's budget. Housing costs, for example, carry significant weight, as they tend to consume a large portion of people's expenses. More on this idea of weight in an upcoming section because it is important for us as investors.

- **Housing and Inflation** - Housing plays a major role in measuring inflation. For homeowners, the CPI uses "owners' equivalent rent," which estimates what a homeowner would pay to rent a similar property. Renters are tracked based on their actual rental payments. Changes in rental prices can significantly impact the overall inflation rate. For real estate investors, rising rents can signal higher revenues but also reflect broader economic inflationary pressures. It's worth noting that since both owners' equivalent rent and actual rents are key components in calculating inflation, when home prices or rents increase, they often contribute directly to a rise in inflation itself. Conversely, when inflation is rising, it is often driven by increases in rents and property values.
- **Imperfect Measurement** - While the CPI and similar metrics are widely used, they are not perfect. No single measure can fully capture every person's experience with inflation. As British statistician George Box famously said, "All models are wrong, but some are useful." The CPI, while an imperfect model, remains useful because it provides a baseline understanding of price trends and cost-of-living changes.
- **Participation Matters** - It's also important to note that not everyone feels inflation the same way. If you don't participate in certain categories of goods or services, their inflation impact may not touch you. For example, if you don't own a car, fluctuations in gasoline prices may

not be as relevant. In housing, if you own your home with a fixed-rate mortgage, rising rental prices won't increase your monthly housing costs, though the broader economic impact of inflation may still affect you in other ways. We will dive much deeper into these dynamics and how to use them to our advantage as real estate investors later. However, for renters, inflation in the housing sector could lead to significantly higher monthly payments.

What Has Inflation Been Historically?

Historically, the average inflation rate in the United States, based on Consumer Price Index (CPI) data from 1914 through 2023, has been approximately 3.27%. On average, this means that the cost of goods and services has risen at this rate annually. It provides a useful baseline for understanding the long-term behavior of inflation.

See Error! Reference source not found. for a chart of historical annual inflation.

The median inflation rate over this same period was 2.75%. This indicates that in half of the years, inflation was below this level, while in the other half, it was higher. The fact that the median is lower than the average suggests that years of high inflation, like those seen during the 1970s and early 1980s, skewed the average upward.

Figure 1

To add further context, the 25th percentile inflation rate was 1.3%, meaning that in one-quarter of the years, inflation was at or below this relatively low level. Conversely, the 75th percentile was 4.625%, indicating that in one-quarter of the years, inflation exceeded this mark. This demonstrates how variable inflation has been in the U.S., ranging from mild price increases to periods of rapid inflation.

In more recent history, from 1980 to 2023, inflation has been slightly lower and more stable with the last few years being an exception that we will discuss below. During this period, the average inflation rate was 3.34%, with a median of 2.9%. This reflects an overall more controlled inflationary environment compared to the larger fluctuations seen in previous decades. While there have still been occasional spikes, inflation has generally been better managed, leading to more predictability for economic planning and investment.

For a broader historical perspective, **Figure 2** from the Inflation entry on Wikipedia illustrates the U.S. inflation rate over several centuries.

I will point out that there were significant instances of negative inflation looking back to the late 1600s through early 1900s.

The Federal Reserve's target inflation rate is 2%. This target aims to create a stable environment for economic growth by balancing price stability and maximum employment. For more information on this policy, visit:

https://www.federalreserve.gov/faqs/economy_14400.htm

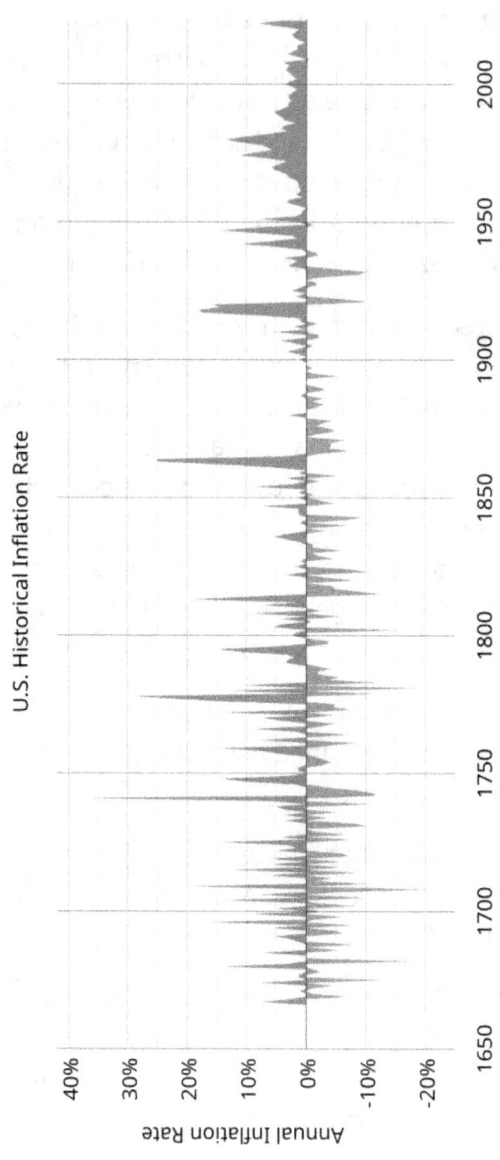

Figure 2

Understanding these historical trends gives real estate investors context and perspective.

Let's see exactly how inflation impacts real estate investors by modeling a variety of real estate investing scenarios in an assortment of inflation environments to see how it changes how you might perform.

Setting Up the Modeling Assumptions

We'll start with my assumptions for creating the models.

These are the baseline assumptions used to simulate how different scenarios may play out over time.

Understanding these assumptions is key to interpreting the results, as they set the stage for modeling a real estate investor's path to financial independence.

- **Modeled for 720 Months (60 Years)** - The models span a 60-year period to capture long-term trends and fluctuations.
- **3% Inflation Rate** - We've chosen a 3% annual inflation rate as our starting point. This figure closely reflects the historical average and provides a solid baseline for our analysis. It's important to note that this rate is a key variable we'll be adjusting to examine how the same investment strategy performs under different inflationary conditions.
- **4% Yearly Safe Withdrawal Rate (SWR)** - The safe withdrawal rate represents the annual percentage of a

retirement portfolio that can be withdrawn without likely depleting the balance over a long period.

- **$10,000 Minimum Target Monthly Income in Retirement (MTMIR) in Today's Dollars/Definition of Financial Independence** - Financial independence is defined as having a minimum target monthly income of $10,000 in today's dollars from investments. This income would come from net cash flow generated by rental properties and from applying the yearly safe withdrawal rate to any amount invested in stocks. Since this target is adjusted upward with inflation, they will often need more than $10,000—sometimes significantly more—depending on how long it takes to reach financial independence. This approach ensures a consistent lifestyle with equivalent buying power, despite changes in inflation over time.

- **$100,000 Starting Account Balance Earning 9.9% Yearly Rate of Return (At Start)** - The initial balance for each scenario is $100,000, invested in stocks. The assumed annual rate of return is 9.9%, reflecting the historical average of the S&P 500 from 1928 to December 21, 2023. This rate will be used for any funds kept in stocks, including money that real estate investors have waiting to deploy into buying properties. It's worth noting that the relationship between stock market returns and inflation is imperfect. There have been periods when the stock market has underperformed during high inflation and times when it has thrived during similar conditions. This recent period of high inflation, for example, saw strong stock market performance.

- **Monthly Income Assumption for Renters** - I assume that in scenarios where people are renting, their combined annual income is $120,000, with each earning $60,000 per year. This translates to an hourly wage of $30 for a standard 40-hour workweek (2,000 hours per year). If they work a full-time job plus a part-time job totaling 60 hours per week (3,000 hours per year), their hourly rate drops to $20. We assume that their income increases with inflation over time. However, in reality, maintaining or increasing their income may require taking on more responsibilities or changing jobs, as wages at the same job may not always keep up with inflation. Returning to the open job market often results in wage increases that match—or even exceed—inflation rates, providing necessary boosts to their earning power.
- **Monthly Expenses** - The assumed monthly expenses, including taxes, are $9,000. This leaves a savings rate of 10%, or approximately $1,000 per month.
- **Home Purchase Assumption (5% Down)** - For scenarios where the individuals are buying an owner-occupant home with 5% down, it's assumed that their monthly savings decrease slightly. This is because buying with just 5% down and Private Mortgage Insurance (PMI) often leads to slightly higher initial costs compared to renting. More on those assumptions when we talk about them buying a property.

These assumptions create a framework to analyze different paths to financial independence for real estate investors, comparing stock market investments, real estate purchases, and other strategies under varying inflation conditions.

Investing in Stocks

Let's start simple and build up more complex models.

If these folks—with the assumptions above—save 10% of their income in stocks earning 9.9% per year in a 3% inflation environment, they would be financially independent in 37.42 years as shown in **Figure 3** and **Figure 4**.

At that point, a 4% safe withdrawal rate from the amount they have invested in stocks would be enough to provide them with $10,000 per month in income adjusted from inflation.

They'd have over $9 million dollars in future, inflated dollars after 449 months. See **Figure 5**.

If we adjust back to today's dollars, it really feels like they have just over $3 million dollars as shown in **Figure 6**.

If inflation was at the Feds target of just 2% per year for the entire 60-year modeling period, they'd achieve financial independence faster as seen in **Figure 7**. How much faster?

With inflation at the Federal Reserve's target of just 2% per year, they would achieve financial independence in 33.58 years compared to 37.42 years under the 3% inflation scenario. This is nearly four years faster, with the only difference being the rate of inflation as shown in **Figure 8**.

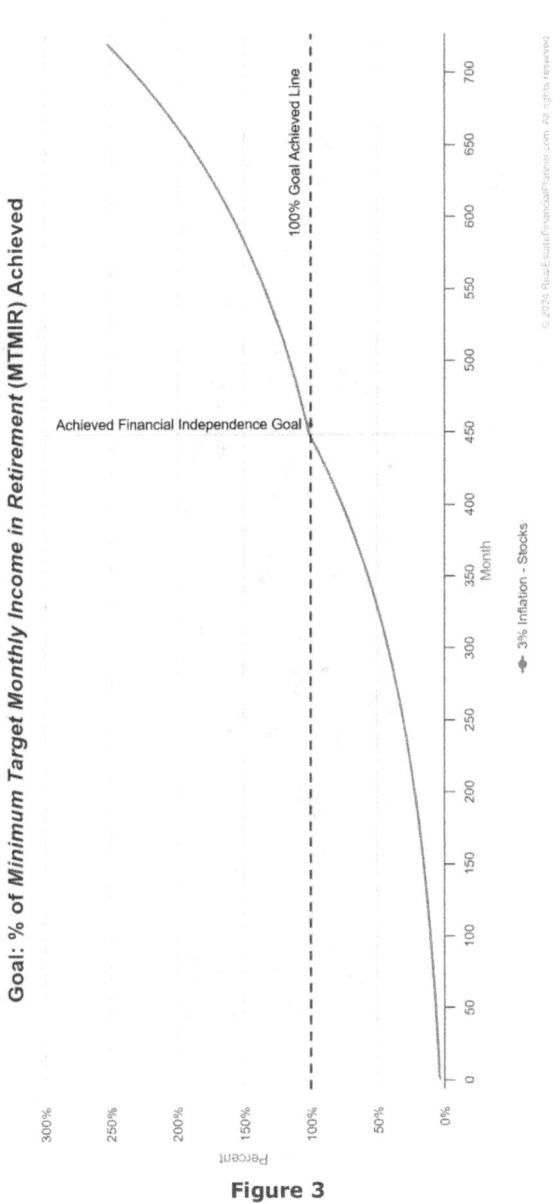

Figure 3

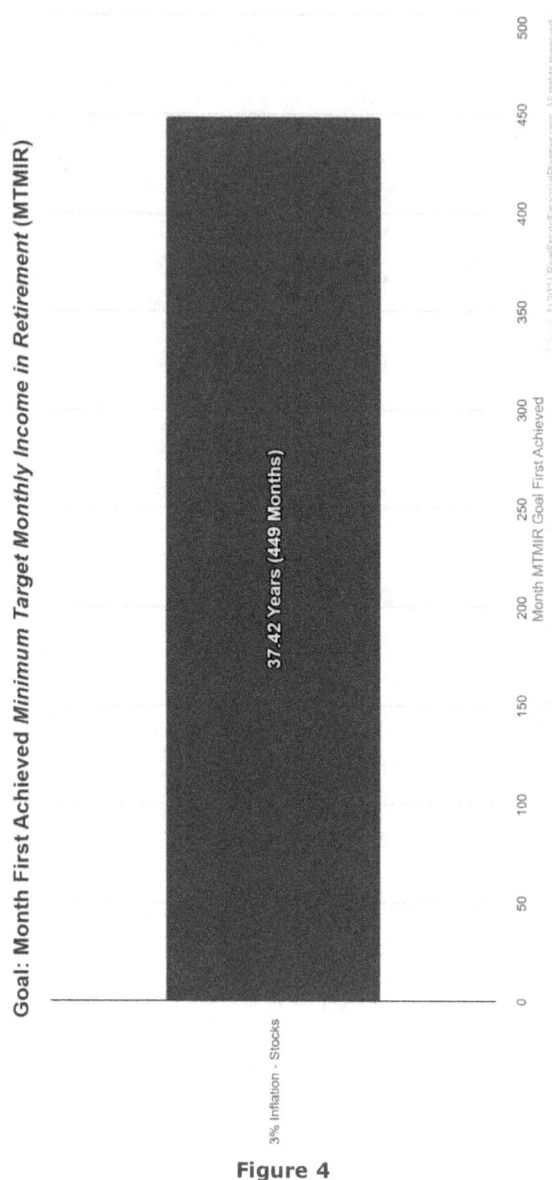

Figure 4

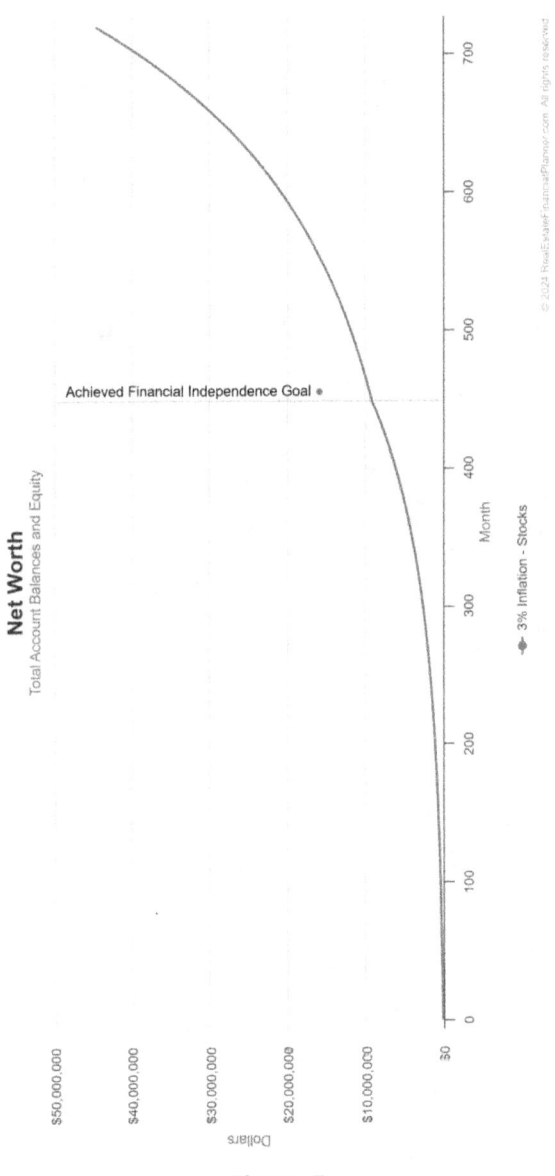

Net Worth
Total Account Balances and Equity

Achieved Financial Independence Goal ●

3% Inflation - Stocks

Month

Dollars

$50,000,000

$40,000,000

$30,000,000

$20,000,000

$10,000,000

$0

Figure 5

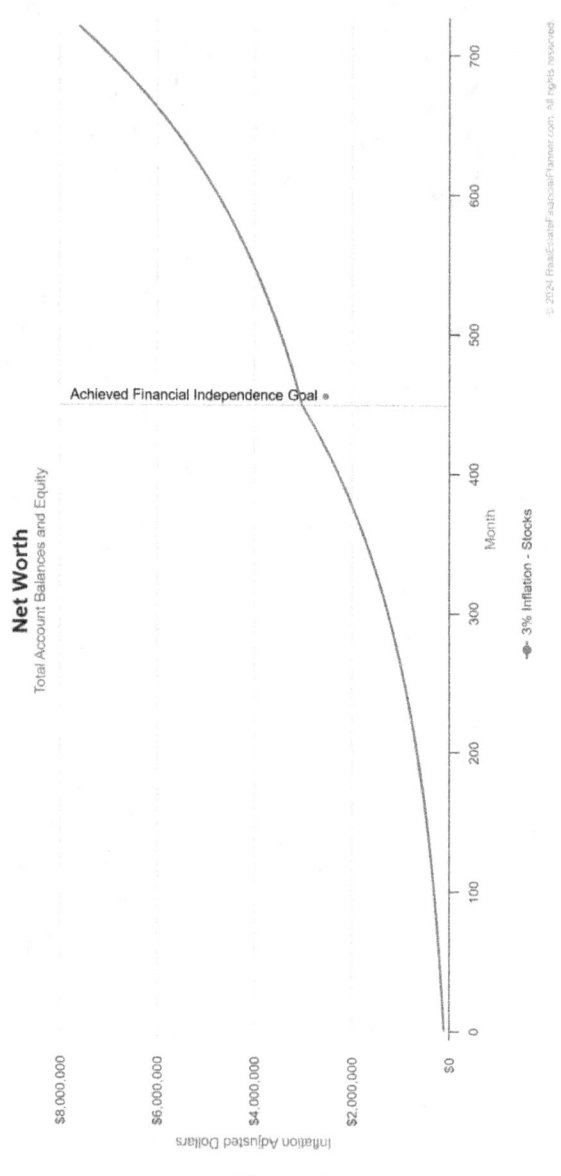

Net Worth

Total Account Balances and Equity

Achieved Financial Independence Goal

3% Inflation - Stocks

Month

Inflation Adjusted Dollars

Figure 6

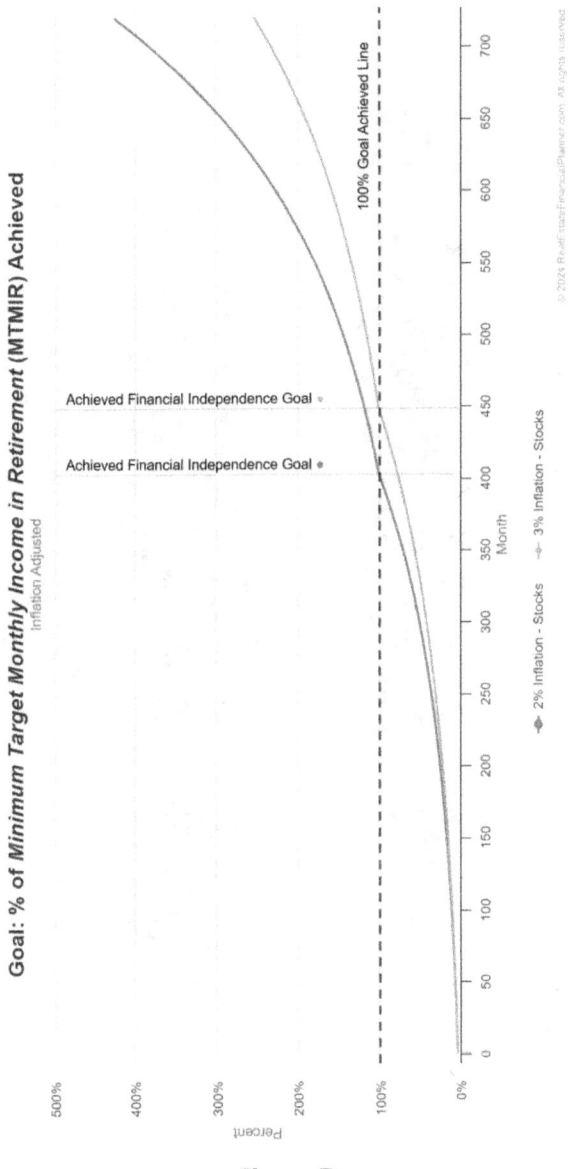

Figure 7

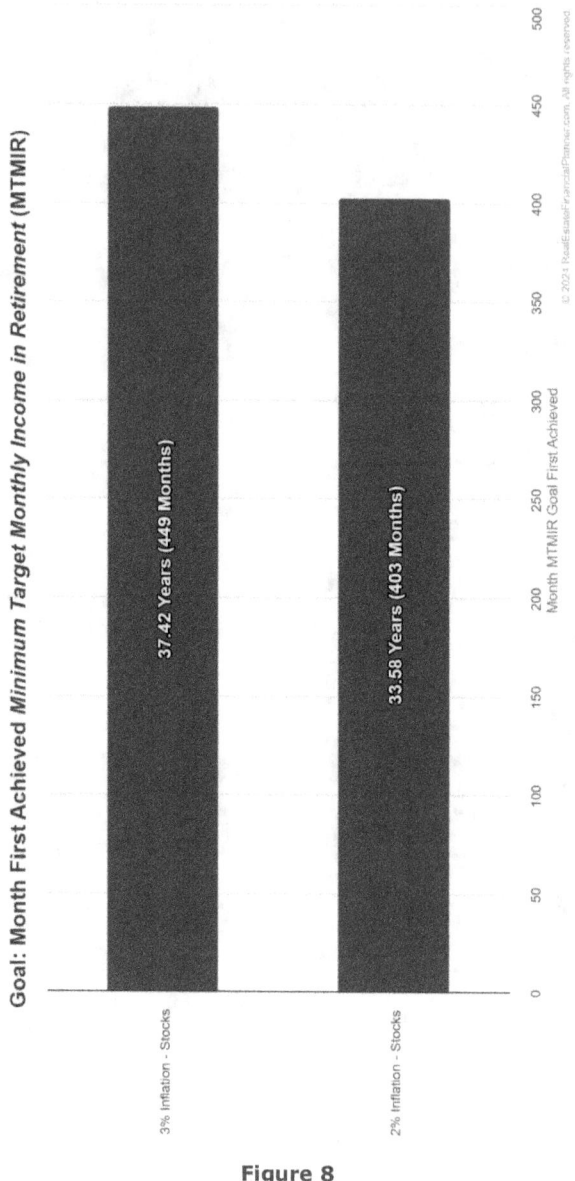

Figure 8

Inflation impacts their path to financial independence in several key ways:

- **Their Income** - Income rises with inflation, meaning that while they earn more in raw dollars over time, their purchasing power remains consistent, preserving their standard of living.
- **Their Expenses** - Just as income grows with inflation, so do their expenses. As the cost of goods and services increases, their overall expenses climb at the same inflation rate, maintaining equilibrium with their rising income.
- **Savings** - Because both their income and expenses increase at the same inflation rate, their savings (set at 10% of their income) also rises. While they are saving more dollars each month in nominal terms, when adjusted for inflation, it equates to the same $1,000 per month in today's dollars.
- **Financial Independence Number** - To maintain their lifestyle in retirement, the income they need from investments must also increase with inflation. The initial target of $10,000 per month in today's dollars grows over time, ensuring they can maintain the same buying power throughout their financial independence journey.

Just Stocks for 4 Inflation Environments

Let's look at 2%, 3%, 4% and 5% inflation environments for the full 60-year modeling period to see how it impacts their ability to be financially independent.

As you can see in **Figure 9**, the higher the inflation rate is the longer it takes for them to achieve financial independence investing solely in stocks.

This, I believe, is what causes some fear and anxiety. If we see high inflation while investing in stocks, and stocks are not always performing better during high inflation periods, it hurts our ability to be financially independent.

With 4% inflation, it takes a little over 42 years to achieve financial independence, which is nearly five years longer than in a 3% inflation environment. This is shown in **Figure 10**.

At 5% inflation, the journey extends to a little over 48 years. This is almost 11 years longer than under a 3% inflation scenario and over six years longer than at 4% inflation. The compounding effect of higher inflation significantly delays the timeline for financial independence.

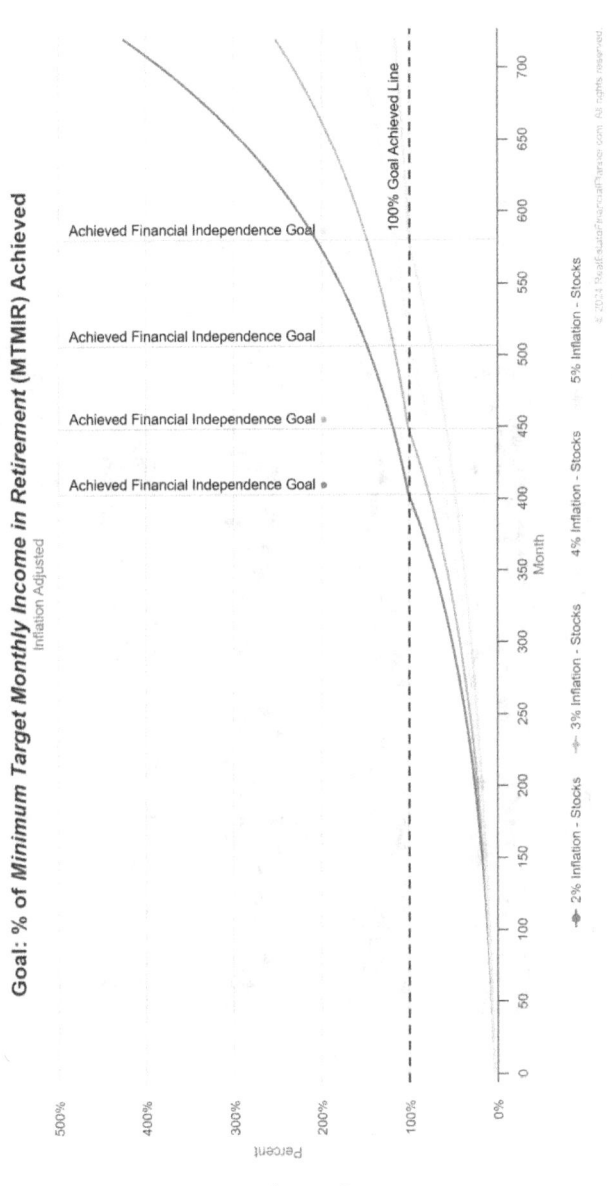

Figure 9

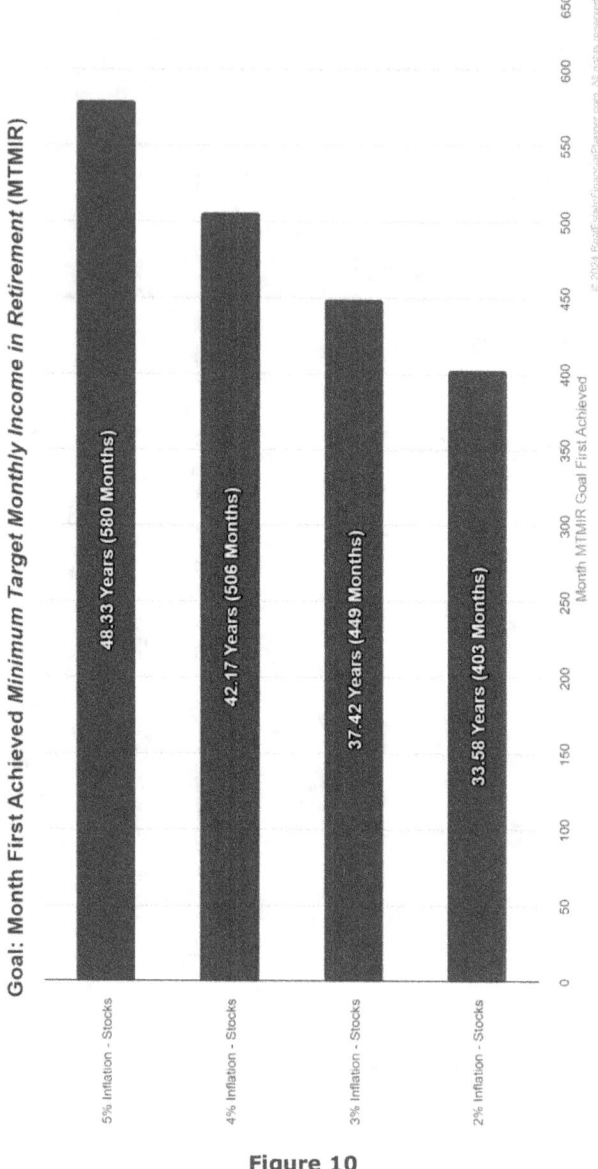

Figure 10

To simplify the modeling, I've ignored the potential impact of social security income. For scenarios with shorter timelines to financial independence, social security typically won't play a significant role in speeding up their financial independence. However, in extended scenarios like those with 5% inflation, individuals may reach the age where they can collect social security before achieving independence solely through investments. In such cases, social security income, combined with their investment income, could push them over the threshold to financial independence more quickly. This is a consideration for longer timelines and high-inflation environments, providing an additional source of stability and income.

Owning a Home versus Renting

Prior to this point, the individuals in our example were renting a home to live in. Deciding to purchase a property has a substantial impact on their financial journey.

To fully appreciate the effect of homeownership on their financial independence, it's important to first understand how inflation impacts the different aspects of owning a home versus renting.

How Inflation Impacts Homeownership Expenses

When you own a home, various expenses are affected by inflation in different ways. Here's a breakdown of key expenses:

- **Principal and Interest on the Mortgage** - If you have a fixed-rate mortgage, the principal and interest portion of your monthly payment does not change with inflation. This stability is one of the key advantages of homeownership during inflationary periods. This will also apply to any investment properties we buy with financing as well, but we'll get to that when we talk about investment properties shortly.
- **Private Mortgage Insurance (PMI)** - PMI is required by lenders when you put down less than 20% of the purchase price on a property. This insurance protects the lender in case you default on the loan, as a smaller down payment represents a higher risk. PMI payments are usually set by the lender and may not be directly affected by inflation. However, once you build up enough equity—typically reaching at least 20% of the home's value—you can usually eliminate this expense on most loans. A notable exception is with FHA (Federal Housing Administration) loans, where PMI (known as a mortgage insurance premium, or MIP) can only be removed through refinancing or paying off the loan entirely.
- **Property Taxes** - Property taxes tend to increase over time as local governments reassess property values or

raise tax rates. Rising home values, often driven by inflation, lead to higher assessed values, which in turn increase property taxes. In our models, we assume that property tax changes are directly tied to how property values change. So, if property values rise quickly due to inflation, property taxes increase at the same inflation rate, creating a direct link between rising market values and higher tax burdens.

- **Homeowner's Insurance** - Insurance premiums tend to increase at inflation rates because they are based on the cost of rebuilding and replacing insured assets, which rise as property values and construction costs go up. Since insurance coverage reflects the value of the property and the cost to repair or rebuild it, we model this in line with property value changes. As property values rise due to inflation, insurance premiums typically increase at the same rate, maintaining consistent coverage relative to the value of the property. On an unrelated note, if insurance companies experience an increase in claims on properties—such as from a rise in the frequency and severity of hurricanes—they may raise insurance premiums faster than inflation. Some markets are currently seeing this trend.

- **Maintenance Costs** - Maintenance and repairs are subject to inflation, as labor and material costs generally rise over time. For example, replacing a roof or repairing plumbing may become more expensive as prices for materials and services increase. In fact, we model maintenance costs as a percentage of rent. Since rent, which is a major component in measuring inflation, typically increases at the inflation rate, maintenance costs also rise accordingly. This ensures that maintenance expenses remain aligned with broader inflation trends in the market.

- **Homeowners Association (HOA) Fees** - HOA fees typically cover insurance, maintenance of common areas, and administrative costs to run the HOA, all of which are impacted by inflation. As the costs for maintaining and insuring common areas and managing the HOA rise due to inflation, HOA fees tend to increase accordingly. We model this by assuming that HOA fees rise at the same inflation rate to reflect these increasing costs.

Here's a quick summary of which homeownership expenses are impacted by inflation and which are not.

Impacted by Inflation:

- **Property Taxes** - Increase as property values rise with inflation.
- **Homeowner's Insurance** - Tied to the value of the property and cost to rebuild, typically increasing with inflation.
- **Maintenance Costs** - Rise due to increasing labor and material costs, often modeled as a percentage of rent.
- **Homeowners Association (HOA) Fees** - Increase as the costs of maintaining and insuring common areas rise with inflation.

Not Impacted by Inflation:

- **Principal and Interest on Fixed-Rate Mortgages** - Remains stable throughout the term of the loan.

- **Private Mortgage Insurance (PMI)** - Generally not tied directly to inflation; set by lenders and can be eliminated once enough equity is built (with some exceptions for FHA loans).

5% Inflation for Homeowner vs Renter

To illustrate how inflation affects homeowners compared to renters, let's break down the expenses over the course of a year and compare a scenario with 5% inflation.

We'll use $10,000 as the total annual cost for homeownership expenses (PITI - Principal, Interest, Taxes, Insurance, HOA fees, PMI, and Maintenance) and $10,000 for annual rent. This will make it easier to see the impact of inflation.

Example for Homeownership

Assume a total annual expense breakdown for a homeowner as follows:

- **Principal and Interest** - $6,000 (fixed, not impacted by inflation)
- **Private Mortgage Insurance (PMI)** - $500 (fixed, not impacted by inflation)
- **Property Taxes** - $1,000 (subject to inflation)
- **Homeowner's Insurance** - $1,000 (subject to inflation)
- **HOA Fees** - $500 (subject to inflation)

- **Maintenance** - $1,000 (subject to inflation)

For a total of $10,000 for the year before a year of 5% inflation.

With a 5% inflation rate:

- **Principal and Interest** - $6,000 (does not change with inflation)
- **PMI** - $500 (does not change with inflation)
- **Property Taxes** - Increase by 5%: +$50 (totaling $1,050)
- **Homeowner's Insurance** - Increase by 5%: +$50 (totaling $1,050)
- **HOA Fees** - Increase by 5%: +$25 (totaling $525)
- **Maintenance** - Increase by 5%: +$50 (totaling $1,050)

For a total new cost of $6,000 (principal and interest) + $500 (PMI) + $1,050 (property taxes) + $1,050 (homeowner's insurance) + $525 (HOA fees) + $1,050 (maintenance) = **$10,175 per year**

The overall increase in total housing cost is $175 due to inflation-affected components, representing a 1.75% increase for the year. This example shows how fixed costs such as principal, interest, and PMI create stability, while inflation-driven increases affect other expenses, leading to a slower rise in total costs compared to renting.

Example for Renting

Assume a total annual rent of $10,000 before a year of 5% inflation.

With a 5% inflation rate:

- **Total Rent** - $10,000 (original cost)
- **Rent Increase** - 5% of $10,000 is +$500 (totaling $10,500)

For a total new cost of **$10,500 per year**.

The overall increase in total housing cost is $500, representing a 5% increase for the year.

Unlike homeownership, where some costs remain stable (principal, interest and PMI), renting is fully subject to inflation-driven increases.

This results in a larger proportional rise in total housing costs compared to homeowners.

This represents just a single year's impact. Now, imagine the compounding effect over 30 years.

Mortgage Payments and Inflation

In summary, inflation offers a unique benefit for homeowners with fixed-rate mortgages. As inflation increases the cost of goods, services, and wages, your mortgage payment remains unchanged. When adjusted for inflation, this means that in "real" terms, your mortgage payment becomes more affordable over time. High inflation further amplifies this effect, making your mortgage payments feel smaller relative to your growing income and the rising costs around you.

I'll illustrate this concept with charts in our modeling, but you heard it here first.

Paying Off Debt with Inflated Dollars

Inflation gradually erodes the value of money, which can work in favor of homeowners with debt. With fixed mortgage payments remaining constant while wages and prices rise, you are effectively paying down your debt with "cheaper" dollars.

I'll provide charts of this effect when we dive into the models.

Financial Independence and Homeownership

Once your mortgage is fully paid off, the amount of income you need to achieve financial independence decreases significantly. This is because your largest housing expense— the mortgage payment—is eliminated.

For example, imagine you need $9,000 per month to cover all your expenses, with $2,000 of that amount going toward principal and interest on your mortgage. While you will still have to cover taxes, insurance, maintenance, and HOA fees, you no longer need the $2,000 you previously allocated to your mortgage payment. This means your monthly financial independence target drops to $7,000.

In contrast, renters face rising housing costs indefinitely as rent prices increase with inflation. This makes achieving financial security more challenging for renters and highlights the unique long-term stability that homeownership can provide in building financial resilience against inflation.

Modeling Owner-Occupant versus Renter

I think it's time I shared with you the model of them buying an owner-occupant property instead of renting.

Here are my assumptions for the property they're buying as an owner-occupant.

- **Using Stock Savings for Purchase** - They're using the money they have saved up in stocks to buy a property to live in. This shifts their assets from stocks to real estate.
- **Property Value and Appreciation** - The property has an initial value and purchase price of $300,000 and appreciates at a rate of 3% per year, which aligns with the assumed inflation rate.
- **Down Payment** - They are making a down payment of 5% of the purchase price, totaling $15,000.
- **Closing Costs** - 1% of the purchase price is allocated for closing costs at the time of purchase, amounting to $3,000.

- **No Seller Concessions** - There are no concessions from the seller to reduce closing costs or other expenses.
- **Mortgage Interest Rate and Term** - The mortgage interest rate is 7.25% with a 360-month (30-year) term, which is standard for residential mortgages.
- **Private Mortgage Insurance (PMI)** - PMI is set at a rate of 0.85% of the initial loan balance. It remains until the loan-to-value ratio drops below 80%, at which point PMI goes away.
- **Vacancy Rate** - A 3% vacancy rate is assumed for rental income scenarios. Since this is a percentage of rent, and rent increases with inflation, the dollar value of the vacancy also rises with inflation.
- **Maintenance Costs** - Maintenance costs are assumed to be 10% of monthly income. As a percentage of rent, this cost increases with inflation, leading to a rising dollar amount over time.
- **HOA Fees** - The property has HOA fees of $500 per year, which increase at a rate of 3% annually, matching inflation. This ensures HOA fees rise in line with broader cost increases.
- **Property Taxes** - Property taxes are assumed to be 0.65% of the property's value per year. For an initial value of $300,000, this amounts to $1,950 per year. Property taxes change as the property value changes with inflation, leading to annual increases.
- **Property Insurance** - Property insurance costs are set at 0.4% of the property's value per year. For a $300,000 property, this equals $1,200 per year initially.

As property values rise with inflation, insurance costs increase accordingly.

And even though they are going to be living in this property, these are the assumptions for when we use the same property as a rental in future modeling:

- **Potential Rent** - If they were to rent out this property, it would generate $2,177.43 per month in rent, with rental income increasing at a rate of 3% per year (matching the assumed inflation rate). While they're living in the property as owner-occupants, this rental rate provides a benchmark for future scenarios.
- **Land Value for Depreciation** - For depreciation calculations (if they rent out the property later), 15% of the purchase price is considered the land value. This affects the depreciation calculation used for tax purposes.

I won't keep you waiting any longer, in a normal 3% inflation environment they achieve financial independence faster by buying an owner-occupant property versus renting. See **Figure 11**.

How much faster?

In **Figure 12**, we see that buying an owner-occupant property allows them to reach their Minimum Target Monthly Income in Retirement (MTMIR) in 34.83 years (418 months), while renting and relying solely on stocks takes 37.42 years (449 months).

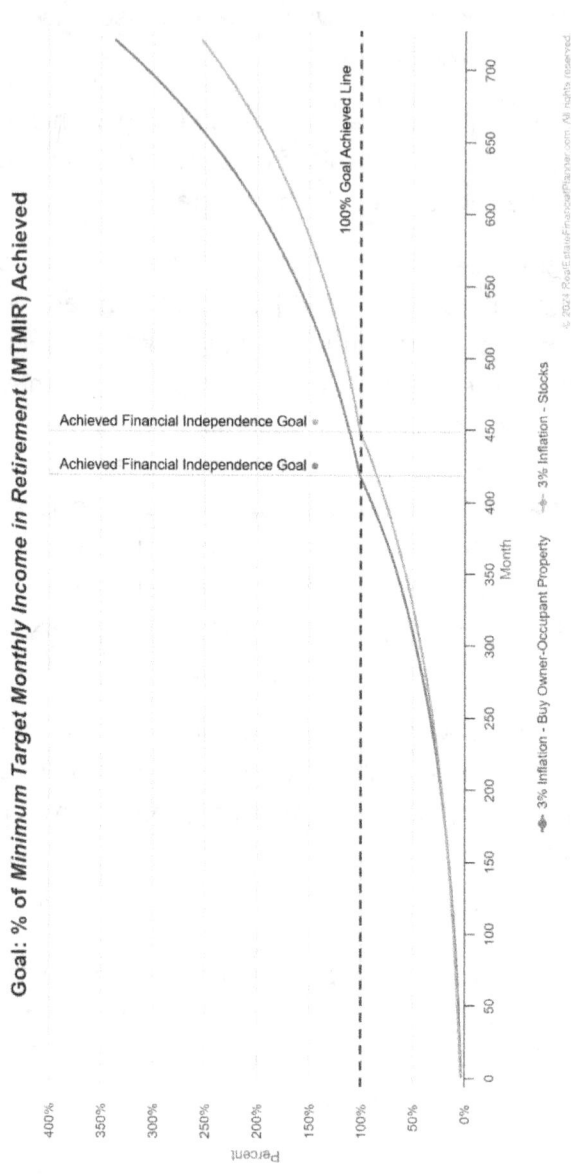

Figure 11

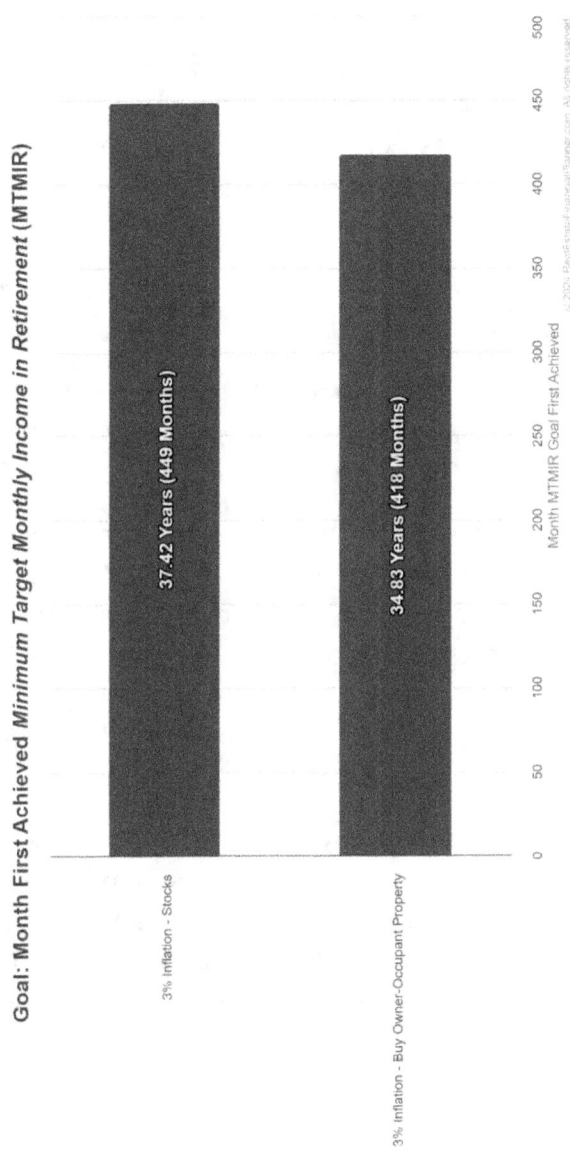

Figure 12

This represents a difference of 2.59 years in a "normal" inflation environment, showing how homeownership, with fixed mortgage payments and potential appreciation, can accelerate the path to financial independence compared to renting.

Now, this is true even though we slightly penalized them for buying the property.

In **Figure 13**, I show how much they're saving from their paychecks in month 2 after they buy an owner-occupant property.

When they were renting, their expenses were about $9,000 per month, allowing them to save $1,002.47 each month. Once they buy a property, their monthly savings drop to $936.25, indicating an additional expense of $66.22 per month as a homeowner. This reflects the increased costs associated with homeownership, including mortgage payments, property taxes, insurance, and maintenance.

But, as you can see in **Figure 14**, it doesn't take long for the rising expenses of renting to surpass the cost of homeownership. This is because the homeowner's mortgage payment (principal and interest) and PMI remain fixed and do not increase with inflation, while rent typically rises over time.

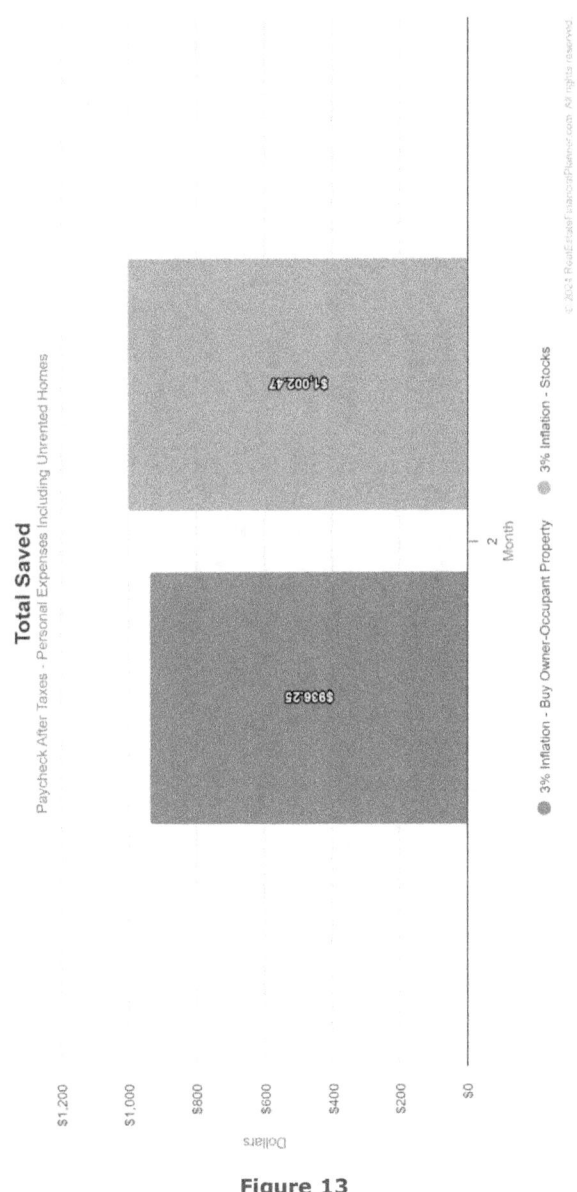

Figure 13

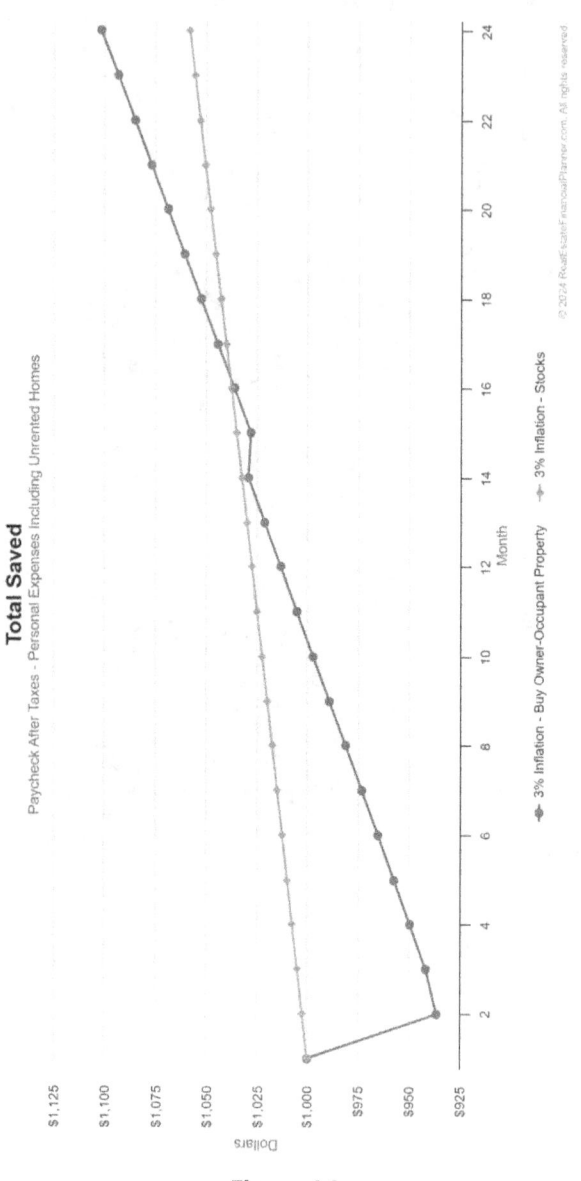

Figure 14

As a result, homeowners eventually have the opportunity to save more than renters. Their stable housing costs allow their savings to grow as rental costs continue to climb, highlighting how homeownership can offer a financial advantage over the long term, particularly as rent inflation drives up housing expenses for renters.

If we compare how much they're saving over the full 60-year modeling period in Error! Reference source not found. I'll point out a few things that are happening:

- In month 360 (30 years into the modeling), the homeowner pays off their mortgage and increases how much they're saving. That's bump up at month 360 in Error! Reference source not found..
- Once they achieve financial independence, they stop working and so their Total Saved goes negative since they are spending from their investments instead of adding to them with job income.
- The amount they go negative increases—from inflation after they achieve financial independence.

If we showed the inflation adjusted version of this, you'd see a different picture. Let's look at that in **Figure 16**.

In **Figure 16** you can see that in inflation-adjusted dollars, the renter is really saving $1,000 per month (in today's dollars) until they achieve financial independence. Then, it drops to -$9,000 per month... the amount of their expenses.

40

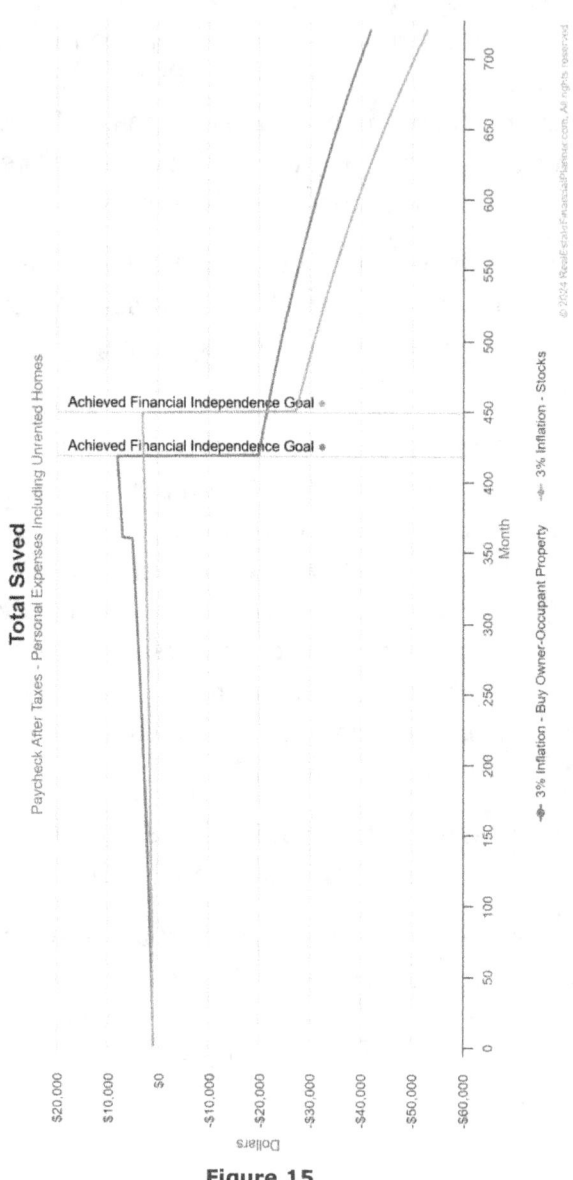

Figure 15

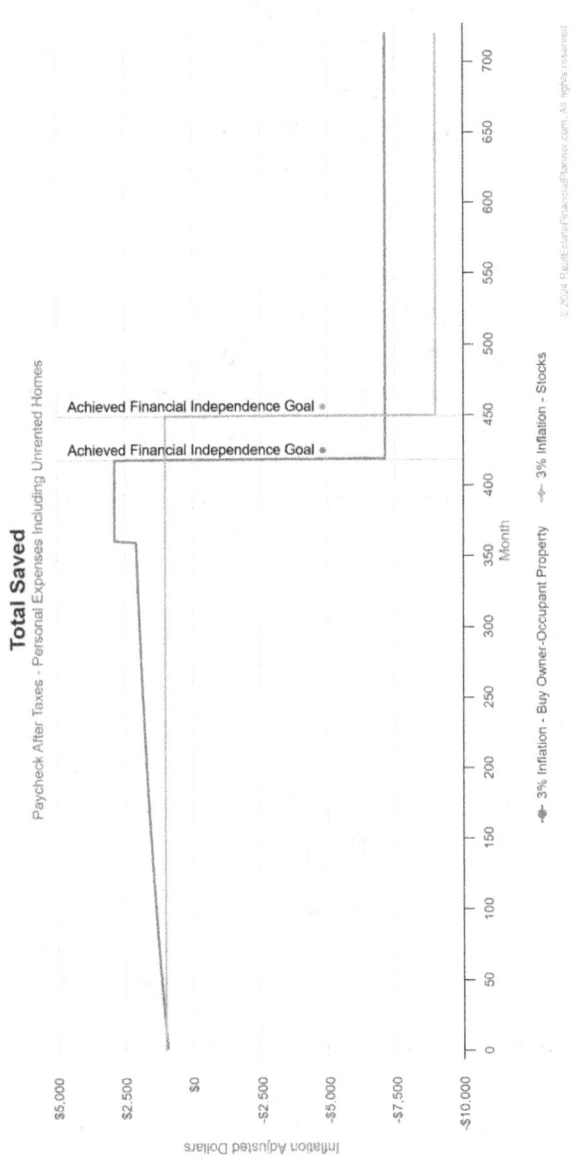

Figure 16

Whereas the homeowner's Total Saved amount is still creeping up—even in inflation-adjusted dollars because that mortgage payment and PMI is fixed. And, when they pay off their mortgage, the amount they're able to save bumps up but remains constant from there until they achieve financial independence.

Once the homeowner achieves financial independence they're at about -$7,122 per month in expenses because they don't have a mortgage anymore. They still have taxes, insurance, HOA, and maintenance on the property but the principal, interest and PMI no longer exist.

Another way to look at this same phenomenon is to look at the total Personal Expenses Including Real Estate as shown in **Figure 17**.

That chart shows how, because of inflation, expenses are increasing over time. And, there's a point at year 30, where the expenses for the homeowner drops a tiny bit when they pay off their house. You can see, by the relative tiny size of the dip though that the mortgage, at that point, is not a significant portion of their expenses.

However, looking at this same chart but as an inflation-adjusted version bringing everything back to today's dollars, the chart looks very different. This is shown in **Figure 18**.

First, because of the scale/zoom, you can see that it was more expensive at first for the owner-occupant. Then, the expenses for the owner-occupant feel less with each passing month from inflation. Until finally, at 30 years, they pay off the mortgage and their expenses drop by the principal and interest portion of their mortgage.

Buying an owner-occupant property also results in a higher net worth as shown in **Figure 19**.

Adjusting the chart of net worth for inflation back to today's dollars in **Figure 20**, you can begin to see the difference in net worth that buying just a single owner-occupant property can have.

In fact, their net worth when they first achieve financial independence as a homeowner in month 418 is almost $9.3 million. Compare that to just under $7.1 million if they rent. That's a difference of over $2.2 million in future, inflated dollars. See this in **Figure 21**.

If we adjust back for inflation to today's dollars, the homeowner has about $3.3 million compared to just over $2.5 million if they rent. That's about an $800K difference just by buying a home to live in and not being subject to the full impact of inflation—even in a historically reasonable 3% inflation rate. That's **Figure 22**.

If you've read any of my other material about why the first $100K is the hardest you know the importance of speed to acquiring an asset base to grow from. They both started with $100K, but buying a home speeds up how long it takes to acquire subsequent chunks of $100K in net worth.

As shown in **Figure 23**, you can see that the homeowner consistently gets to their next $100K faster than the renter through the first million.

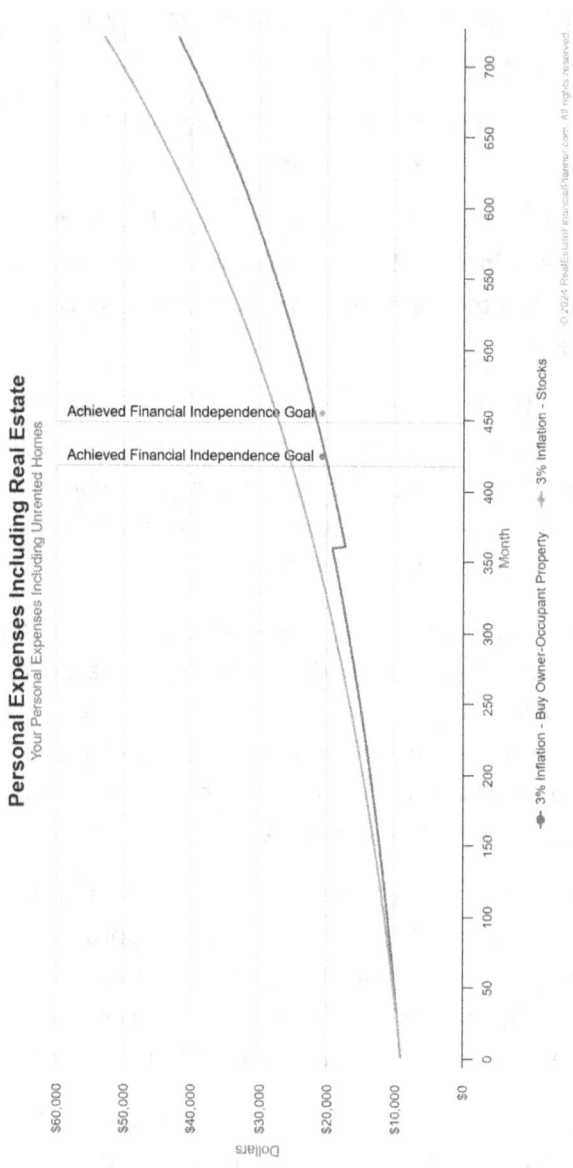

Figure 17

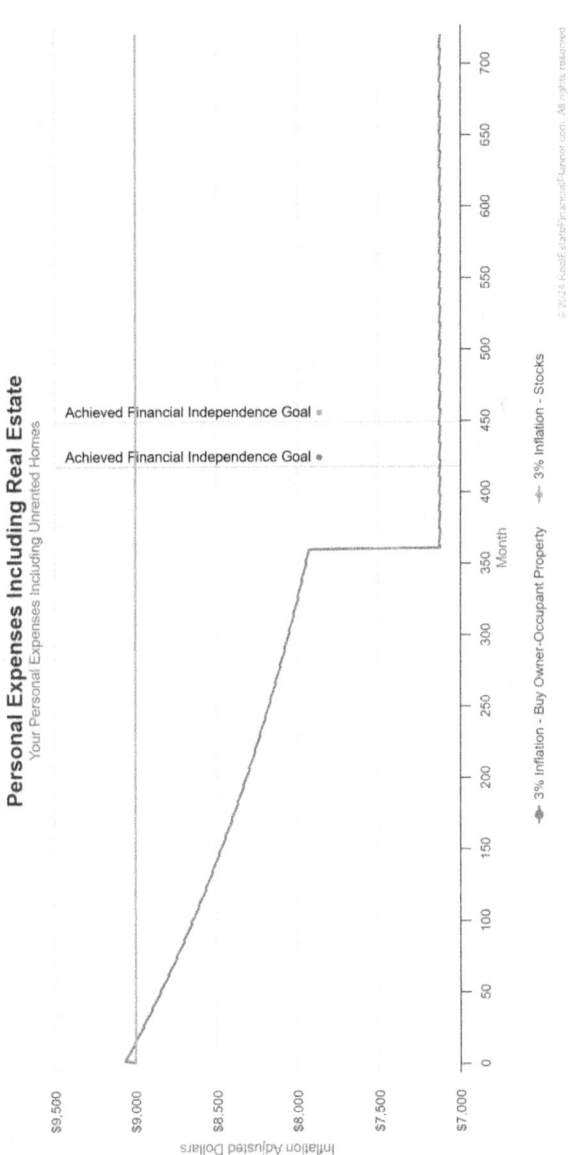

Figure 18

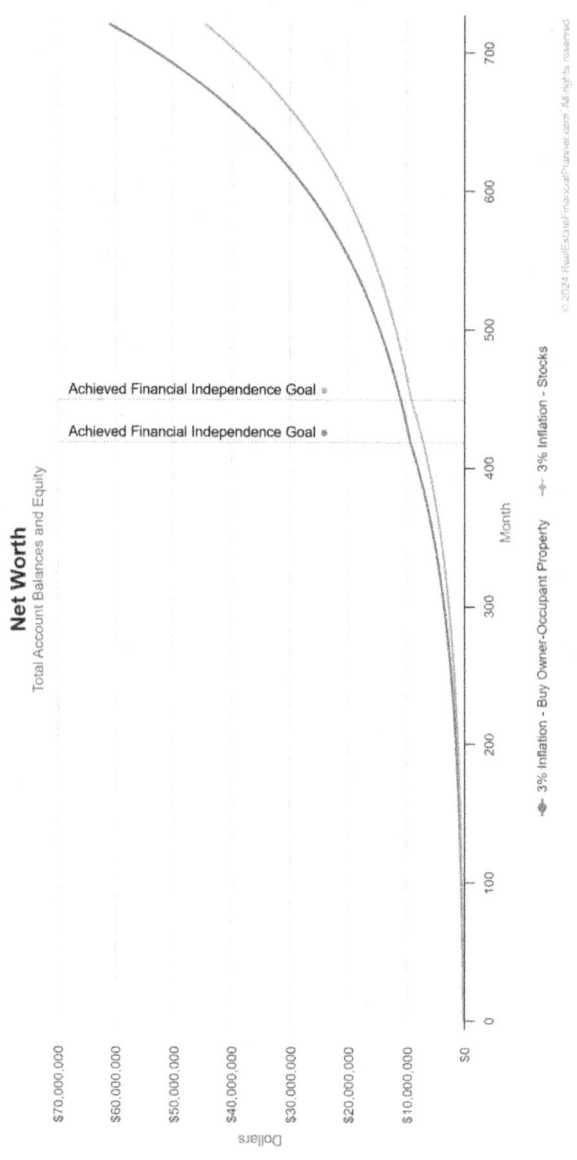

Figure 19

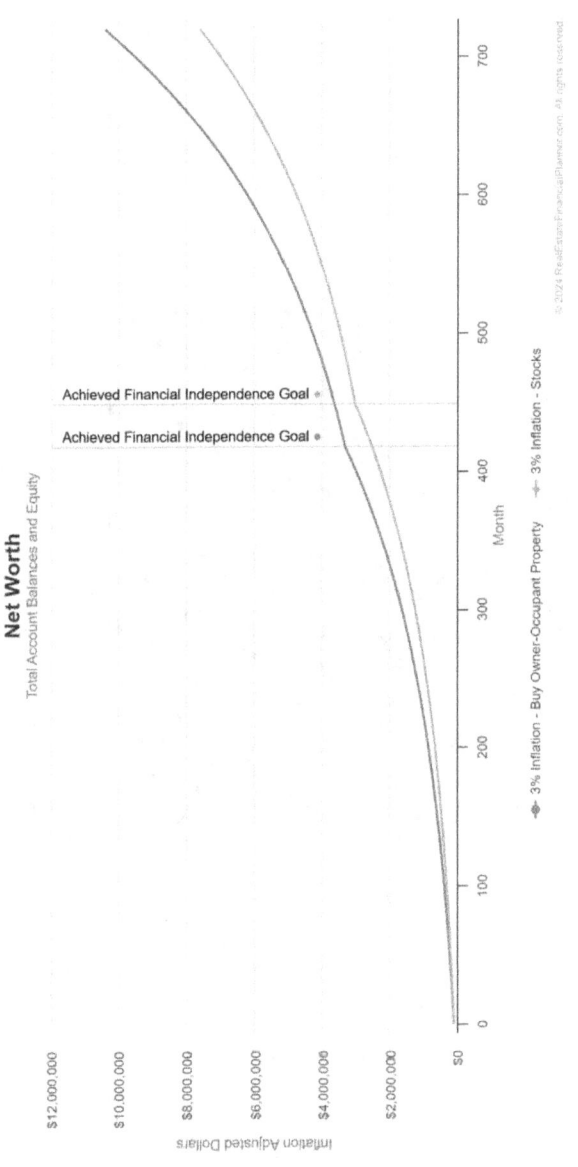

Figure 20

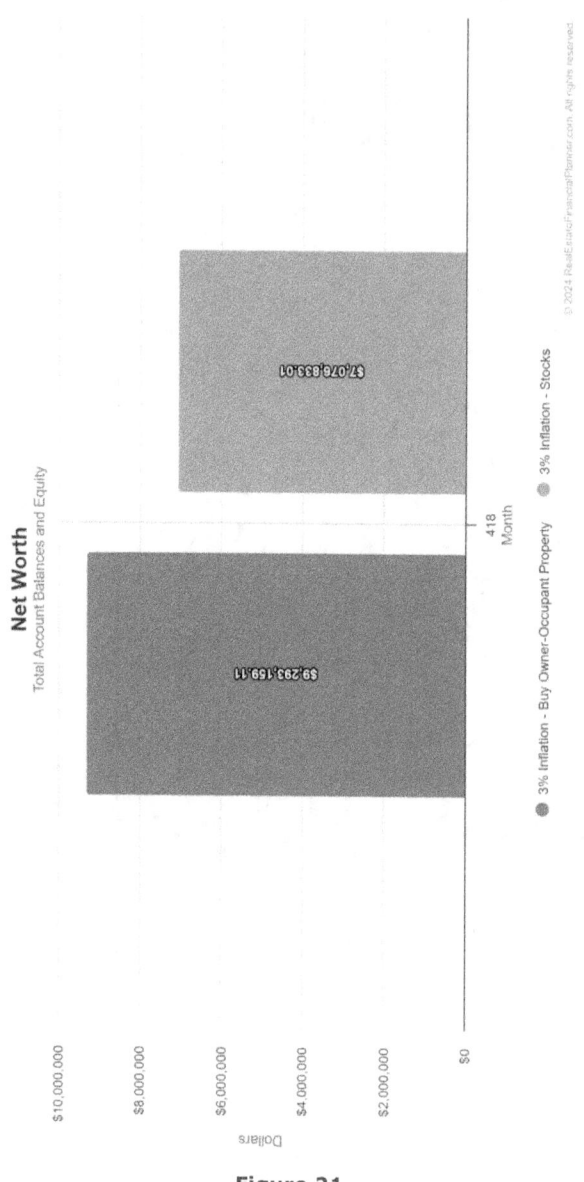

Figure 21

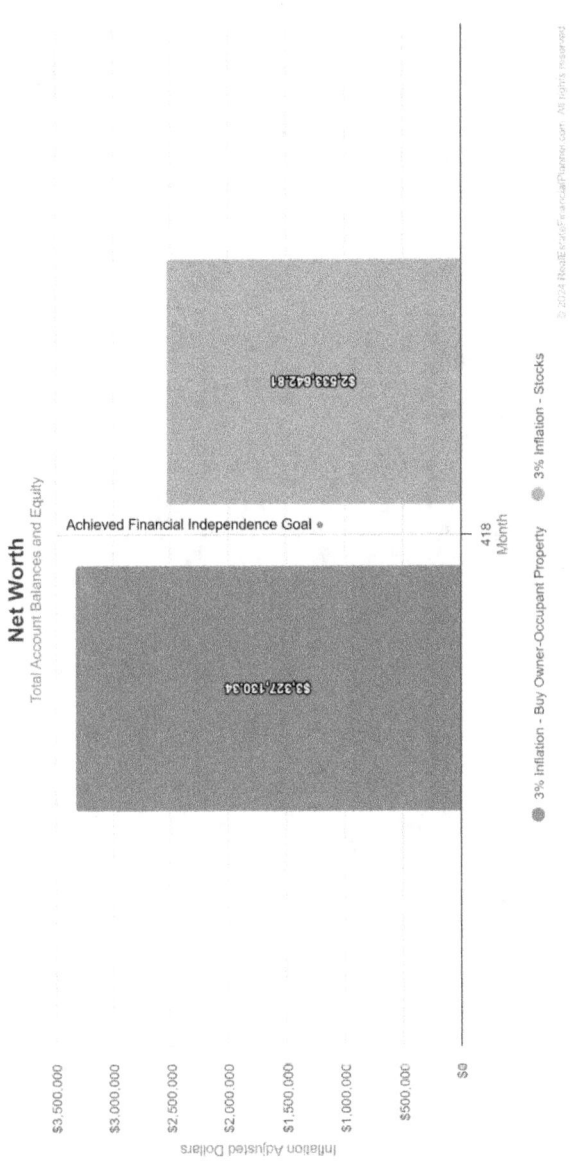

Figure 22

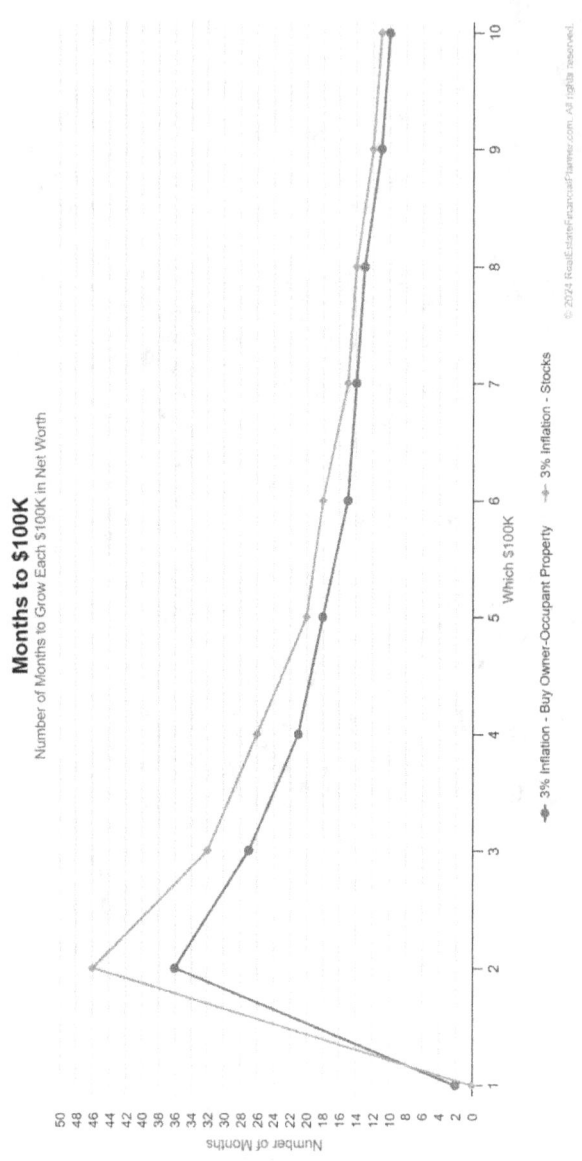

Figure 23

Before we continue with our modeling of inflation, let's take a brief tangent to discuss how interest rates are related to inflation.

Interest Rates and Inflation

Interest rates and inflation have a complex, closely interconnected relationship that plays a significant role in economic policy. The Federal Reserve (the Fed) adjusts interest rates as a primary tool to influence inflation and maintain economic stability.

The Role of the Federal Reserve

Adjusting Interest Rates Up or Down - The Federal Reserve raises or lowers interest rates to control inflation and stabilize the economy. By adjusting these rates, the Fed aims to either encourage or slow down economic activity.

How Interest Rate Changes Affect Inflation

- **Raising Interest Rates to Curb Inflation** - When the Fed raises interest rates, borrowing becomes more expensive for both businesses and individuals. Higher interest rates lead to increased costs for loans, mortgages, and other forms of debt. As a result, spending and investment typically decrease, cooling demand for goods and services. Lower demand tends to slow price increases, thereby curbing inflation.

- **Lowering Interest Rates to Encourage Inflation** -
Conversely, when the Fed lowers interest rates,
borrowing becomes cheaper. This reduces the cost of
loans for home mortgages, business expansions, and
consumer credit, which encourages spending and
investment. More money flowing through the economy
often increases demand for goods and services, putting
upward pressure on prices and, in turn, raising inflation.

COVID-19 and Government Responses

During the COVID-19 pandemic, world leaders, including
those in the United States, provided direct financial support
to citizens through stimulus checks and other measures. This
was not limited to one political party; both major parties in
the U.S. contributed to stimulus efforts during their terms.
These measures aimed to provide immediate relief in the
face of unprecedented economic disruption.

I want to emphasize that this was not just something the US
did. Other countries provided financial support to its citizens
as well.

Economics 101: Money Supply and Inflation

- **Increasing the Money Supply** - When the money
supply increases, demand for goods and services tends
to rise because people have more money to spend.
However, if supply does not keep pace with demand,

prices increase, causing inflation. During COVID-19, supply chain issues and labor shortages further exacerbated this dynamic, as fewer goods and services were available.

- **Labor Shortages and Wage Increases** - COVID-related financial support temporarily discouraged some workers from returning to lower-paying jobs, contributing to labor shortages. To attract workers, some businesses had to raise wages. This increased their costs, which were often passed on to consumers through higher prices.

- **Global Inflationary Pressures** - Much of the financial relief during COVID-19 was financed through government debt, which can lead to increased money printing and further inflationary pressures. Since these issues were global, inflation affected both domestic and imported goods and services worldwide.

The Fed's COVID Response

To cushion the economic impact of COVID-19, the Fed lowered interest rates to near-zero levels. This move aimed to prevent a deep recession by making borrowing cheaper for businesses and individuals, thus stimulating spending and investment. However, this influx of dollars into the economy, combined with supply chain disruptions, increased demand and pushed up prices, contributing to inflation.

Complex and Imperfect Systems

Adjusting interest rates to manage inflation is not a precise science. These systems are complex, slow-moving, and often imperfect. The Fed makes adjustments and then monitors the effects over time, making further changes as needed to stabilize the economy. It is challenging (read that as near impossible) to know the *exact impact* of these changes in advance. They make an educated guess and then check the results in the economy.

Money Supply and Inflation

If we look at a chart comparing inflation (CPI Index) to the M2 Money Supply (a measure of the money circulating in the economy), you can see that they often move in the same direction—when there's more money circulating, inflation tends to rise.

When there is a large increase in the amount of money flowing through the economy, it can lead to higher demand for products and services, which in turn causes prices to rise. You can see this pattern reflected in **Figure 24** which is from the Inflation entry for Wikipedia.

The U.S. government's response to the economic challenges of COVID-19 included flooding the economy with money through stimulus checks, emergency loans, and by lowering interest rates that were already very low.

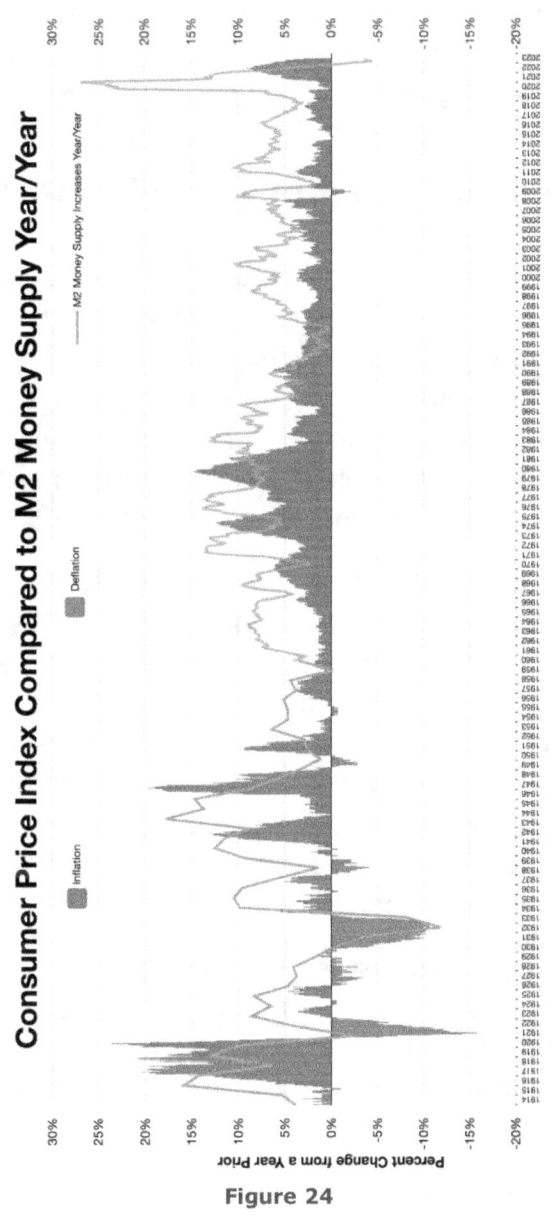

Figure 24

This increase in the money supply contributed to a rise in inflation, as shown in the graph. It illustrates how more money circulating in the economy can push prices higher.

Why a 2% Inflation Target Matters

The Fed aims for a 2% target inflation rate to strike a balance between price stability and economic growth. Negative inflation (deflation) or zero inflation can be harmful, as they may lead to reduced consumer spending and investment, causing economic stagnation. A small, steady rate of inflation encourages economic activity, fosters stable price growth, and helps prevent the adverse effects of deflation.

So, while it might initially seem desirable for prices to decrease (negative inflation), this can have serious negative consequences. For example, when consumers expect prices to continue falling, they may delay purchases, reducing demand and slowing economic growth. Businesses, in turn, may cut back on production and investment, leading to job losses and further economic contraction. This self-reinforcing cycle can be challenging to break and can lead to long-term economic stagnation.

I am giving you this basic economics primer solely to give us a shared background for discussing real estate. If you're really interested in this topic, seek out books, courses, podcasts and videos on economics. Economics is not my area of expertise.

Now, let's get back to some real estate investor modeling.

Homebuyers In Various Inflation Environments

After that brief economics detour, let's get back to the impact of buying a home to live in on various inflationary environments.

Figure 25 illustrates how long it takes to achieve financial independence under different inflation scenarios over a 60-year modeling period for pairs of renting (stocks-only) versus buying an owner-occupant property.

Here's a breakdown of each pair and the difference in time to financial independence:

- 5% Inflation (Stocks) vs. 5% Inflation (Buy Owner-Occupant Property)

  - *Stocks:* 48.33 years (580 months)
  - *Buy Owner-Occupant Property:* 40.42 years (485 months)
  - *Difference:* Buying a home results in financial independence 7.91 years (95 months) sooner if inflation remains at 5% annually.

- 4% Inflation (Stocks) vs. 4% Inflation (Buy Owner-Occupant Property)

  - *Stocks:* 42.17 years (506 months)
  - *Buy Owner-Occupant Property:* 37.25 years (447 months)
  - *Difference:* Buying a home leads to financial independence 4.92 years (59 months) faster.

- 3% Inflation (Stocks) vs. 3% Inflation (Buy Owner-Occupant Property)

  - *Stocks:* 37.42 years (449 months)
  - *Buy Owner-Occupant Property:* 34.83 years (418 months)
  - *Difference:* Buying a home achieves financial independence 2.59 years (31 months) earlier.

- 2% Inflation (Stocks) vs. 2% Inflation (Buy Owner-Occupant Property)

  - *Stocks:* 33.58 years (403 months)
  - *Buy Owner-Occupant Property:* 32.92 years (395 months)
  - *Difference:* Buying a home allows for financial independence 0.66 years (8 months) sooner.

In every scenario, purchasing an owner-occupant property accelerates the path to financial independence compared to renting and relying solely on stocks. This demonstrates how homeownership can be a more effective hedge against inflation, offering stability and cost predictability over time.

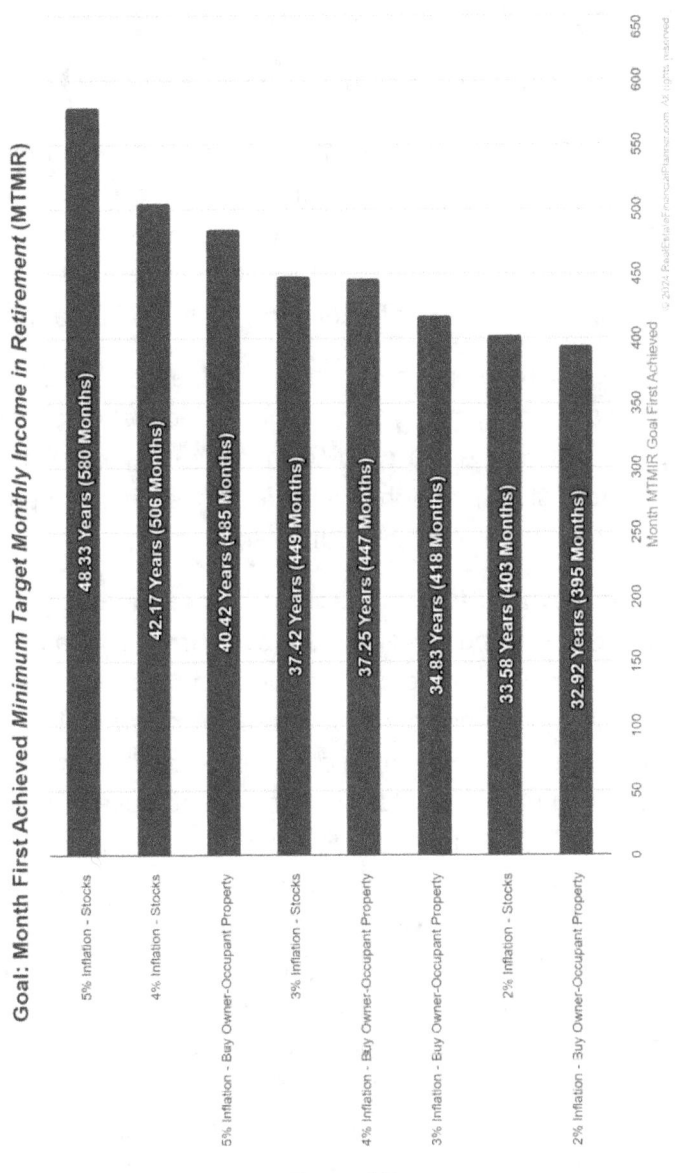

Figure 25

Paying Off Mortgages Early in a High Inflation Environment

In a high inflation environment, paying off your mortgage early might seem like a good idea, but there are strong reasons to reconsider. High inflation erodes the real value of money over time. This means that future mortgage payments, made with inflated dollars, cost less in real terms.

Fixed-rate mortgage payments also provide stability as other prices rise, making your debt effectively cheaper. Additionally, using extra cash to invest rather than paying off low-interest debt might yield better returns, given the potential growth in high-inflation scenarios.

- **Paying with "Cheaper" Dollars** - Inflation decreases the purchasing power of money over time. This means that as wages and the cost of goods increase, the dollars you use to pay your mortgage remain the same in nominal terms but become cheaper in "real" terms. Continuing to pay off debt with devalued dollars allows you to maintain more buying power and reduces the true cost of your mortgage over time.
- **Fixed Payments Provide Stability** - Fixed-rate mortgages lock in your principal and interest payments, shielding them from inflation's effects. While other expenses may rise due to inflation, your monthly mortgage payment remains constant. This stability means that, relative to your rising income and other costs, your mortgage payment becomes a smaller portion of your overall expenses, making it financially

advantageous to carry this type of debt in an inflationary environment.

- **Opportunity Cost of Paying Down Debt** - Choosing to pay off your mortgage early in a high inflation environment comes with opportunity costs. Extra cash that could be used to pay down debt might instead be invested in assets with a higher rate of return than your mortgage interest rate. Stocks, real estate (as we'll do more modeling of shortly), and other investments may offer inflation-driven growth, potentially providing a better return on investment than reducing low-interest mortgage debt.

I feel like I'm repeating myself, but the point here is important to be repeated: when inflation is high, the real cost of debt declines. Fixed-rate mortgages offer stability, making it financially advantageous to hold onto this debt while prices rise.

Rather than paying off your mortgage early, it might be more beneficial to direct your cash toward investments with greater growth potential. This strategy allows you to leverage inflation while maintaining financial flexibility.

Now that I've said all that, realize there are times when paying off a mortgage—like to push you over the edge of being financially independent, to reduce risk, to change your asset allocations, or to help qualify for a new purchase— might still make a lot of sense.

Nomad™

Nomading is the sequential buying of owner-occupant properties where you keep the previous property you lived in as a rental.

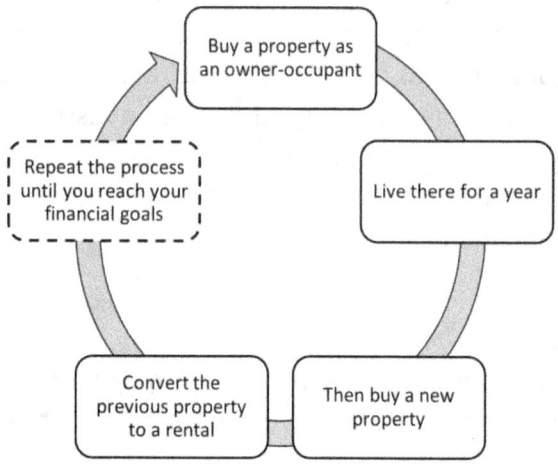

Basically:

- You buy a property as a owner-occupant (like we just did in previous modeling). This is often done with low down or nothing down loans with lower, owner-occupant mortgage interest rates. And, if you're putting less than 20% down, you'll likely have PMI.
- You live there for a year. This is a requirement of the lender. Failing to do so is considered loan fraud and has severe consequences (severe like possible prison time severe).
- After you fulfil the obligation of the lender, you then buy another owner-occupant property with little or nothing

down (usually 5%) to live in and move into that new property to live there for at least a year.

- You convert the previous property you were living in to a rental after you move out.
- You repeat this process until you reach your financial goals and have the number of rental properties you desire.

By utilizing this strategy you're able to acquire a portfolio of rental properties with small down payments (or no down payment in some rarer cases) and better, owner-occupant interest rates.

You could buy about 4 times as many properties with the same down payment—instead of needing 20% down for each property, you could buy 4 properties with the same 20% down payment instead.

For more detailed information about the Nomad™ real estate investing strategy, check out *Introduction to Nomad™ Real Estate Investing* (and other titles) in *The Real Estate Investing Mentor* series.

What if instead of just buying one owner-occupant property, they decide to Nomad™ and acquire 9 rentals and an owner-occupant property to live in (10 properties total over about 10 years)?

Nomad™ at 3% Inflation

Let's first start the modeling by comparing just the 3% inflation environment and dig into that then we can look at summaries for how Nomad™ performs in a variety of inflationary environments.

As you can see in **Figure 26**, of the options we've consider so far (renting and just investing in stocks, buying a single owner-occupant property and otherwise investing in stocks and now Nomading™), the Nomad™ strategy takes only 28.33 years to be financially independent.

That's about 6.5 years faster than just buying a single property to live in and over 9 years faster than renting and investing in stocks.

Not only is Nomad™ faster to achieve financial independence, but it also allows them to live at a higher standard of living from their investments once they are financially independent as shown in **Figure 27**.

In fact, by the time they'd be just barely financially independent by renting and investing in stocks in month 449, they'd be able to live at twice that standard of living if they had Nomaded™ at that month. So, instead of it feeling like they were able to safely spend $10K per month, they could safely spend a little over $20K per month as a Nomad™ at that point. This is shown as a zoomed in chart into month 449 in **Figure 28**.

How quickly are they acquiring properties when they Nomad™? In **Figure 29** we can see that it takes 195 months (or a little over 16.25 years) to acquire all 10 properties.

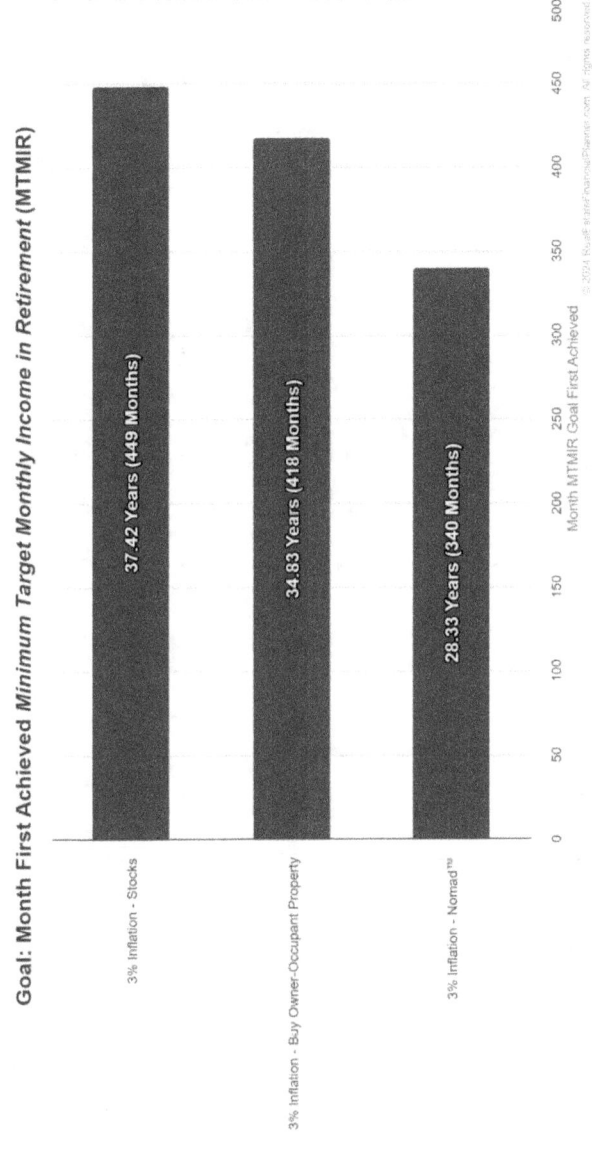

Figure 26

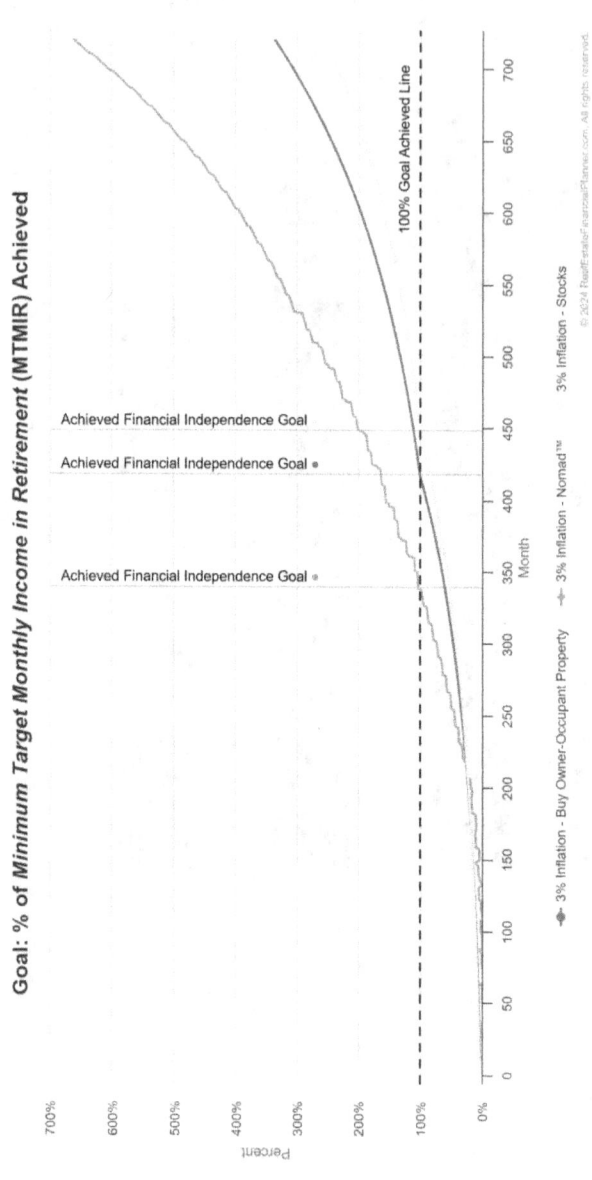

Figure 27

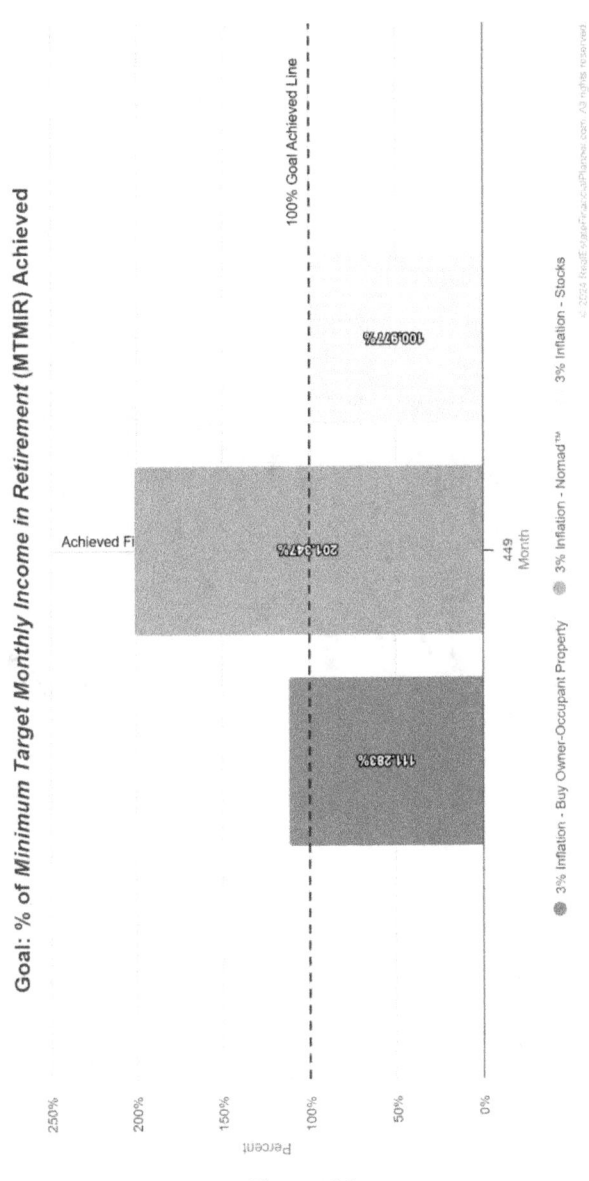

Figure 28

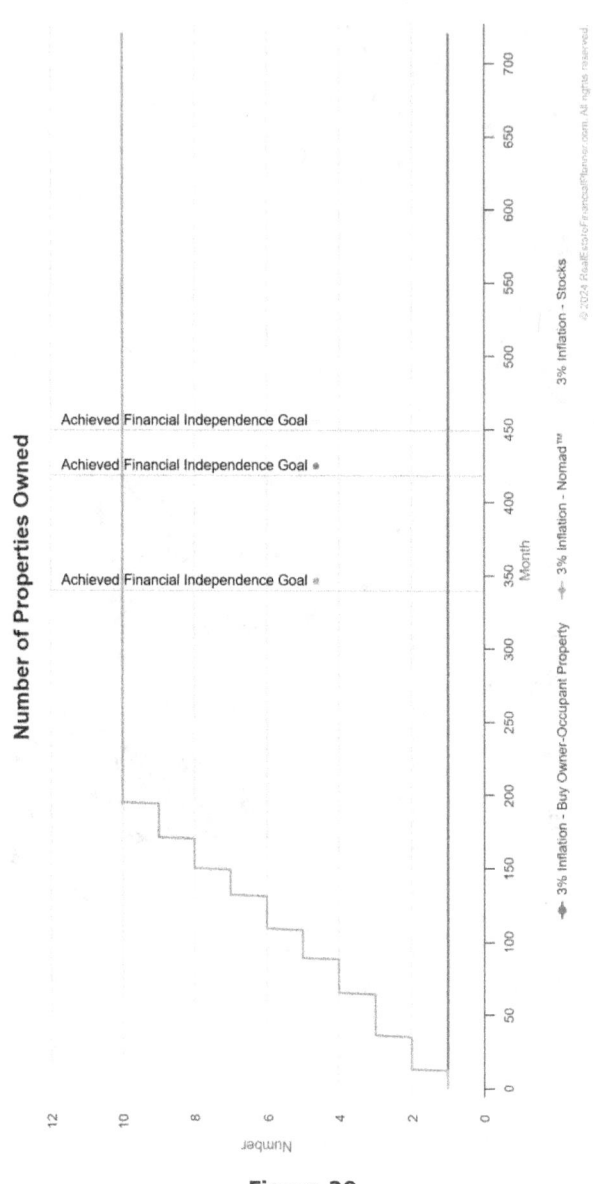

Figure 29

Why weren't they able to do it in exactly 10 years (120 months)? Was it:

- Not able to save down payment, closing costs, and reserves quickly enough?
- Not able to qualify for the loans from their debt-to-income?

If we zoom in on their account balance for the acquisition period (195 months) in **Figure 30**, we can see that they have plenty of money for down payments.

If we adjust back for inflation to today's dollars, you can get a feel for how close to their original $100K they are during that period in **Figure 31**.

So, maybe they're acquisition speed is being limited by keeping their debt-to-income low enough to qualify for more loans putting only 5% down.

In **Figure 32**, you can see their debt-to-income over the entire 60-year modeling period. And it does look like when they're Nomading™ they are pushing up against the 45% debt-to-income limit to be able to get new loans that we set as part of their criteria.

As an aside, the bump up when they reach financial independence at month 340 on the chart is when they stop working and their income from their job goes to zero. They're not trying to qualify for more loans at that point. You can see this a bit clearer in the zoomed in version in **Figure 33**.

So, how much did income did they require to be able to buy 10 properties as a Nomad™? In raw, inflated dollars it is just over $15,000 they had to be earning about 16 years from when they started assuming they had no other debt besides the properties. You can see this in **Figure 34**.

However, if you adjust back for inflation to today's dollars in **Figure 35** you can see it is the same $10,000 we assumed at the beginning.

Their personal expenses including the cost of their owner-occupant property is highest when they rent and invest in stocks as we previously discussed in detail. As you can see in **Figure 36**, renting is more expensive than doing the Nomad™ strategy and buying a new property to live in about every year. The least expensive personal expenses is just buying that one owner-occupant property and living in that forever.

It is even easier to see if we take the same chart and adjust for inflation back to today's dollars in **Figure 37**. Their personal expenses as a renter remains steady at that $9,000 per month. Whereas the expenses for buying the owner-occupant property has a pretty steady decline until they pay off the mortgage and then drops to about $7,100 per month. With the Nomad™ model, they keep bumping it up each time they buy a new property slightly above what it costs to rent, but once they reach that 10th property the same curve we saw when they just bought an owner-occupant property returns including the drop when they pay off that last mortgage.

Total Account Balances

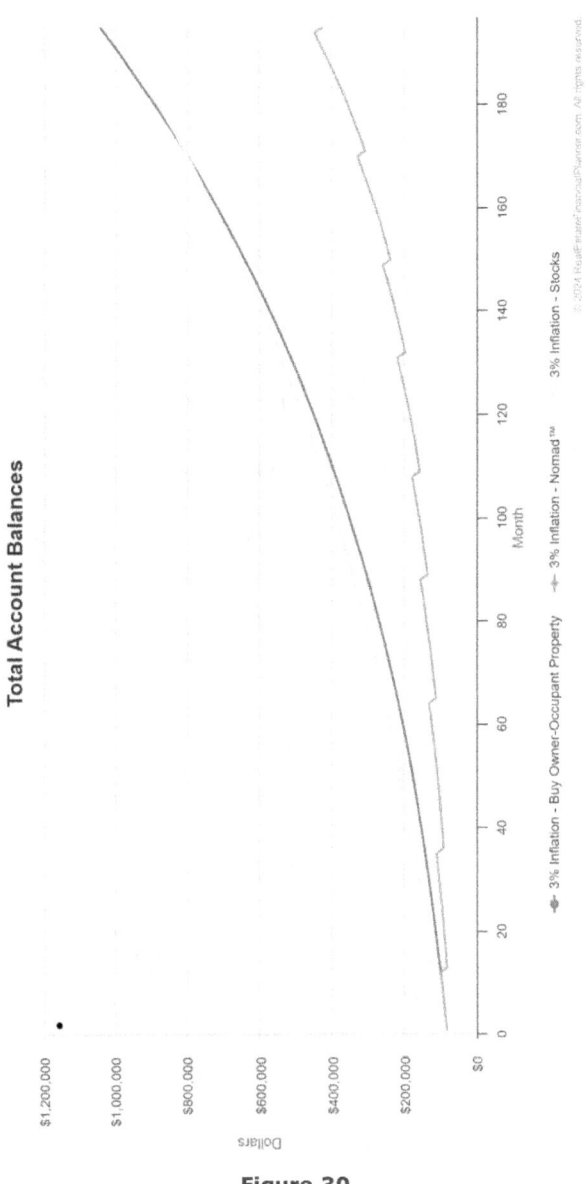

Figure 30

72

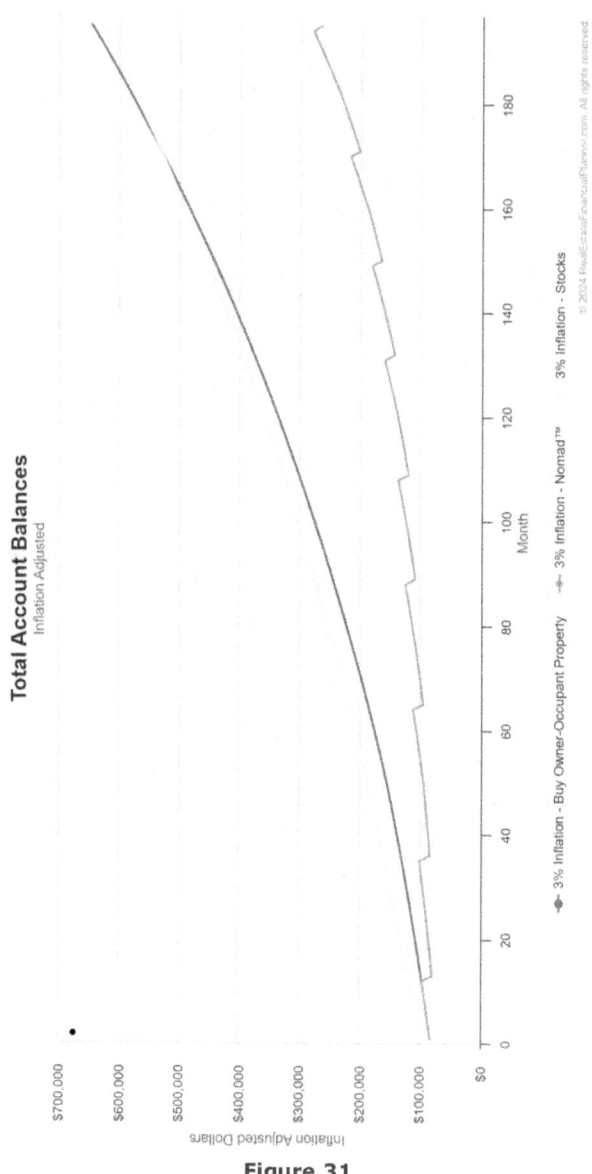

Figure 31

© 2024 James Orr. All rights reserved.

Debt-To-Income

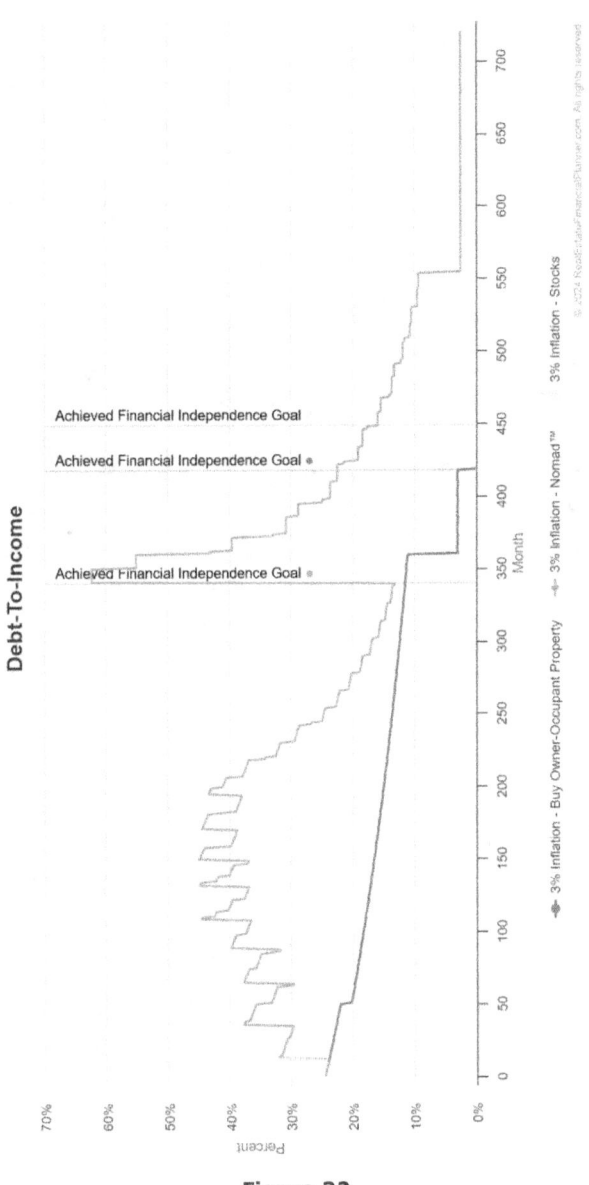

Figure 32

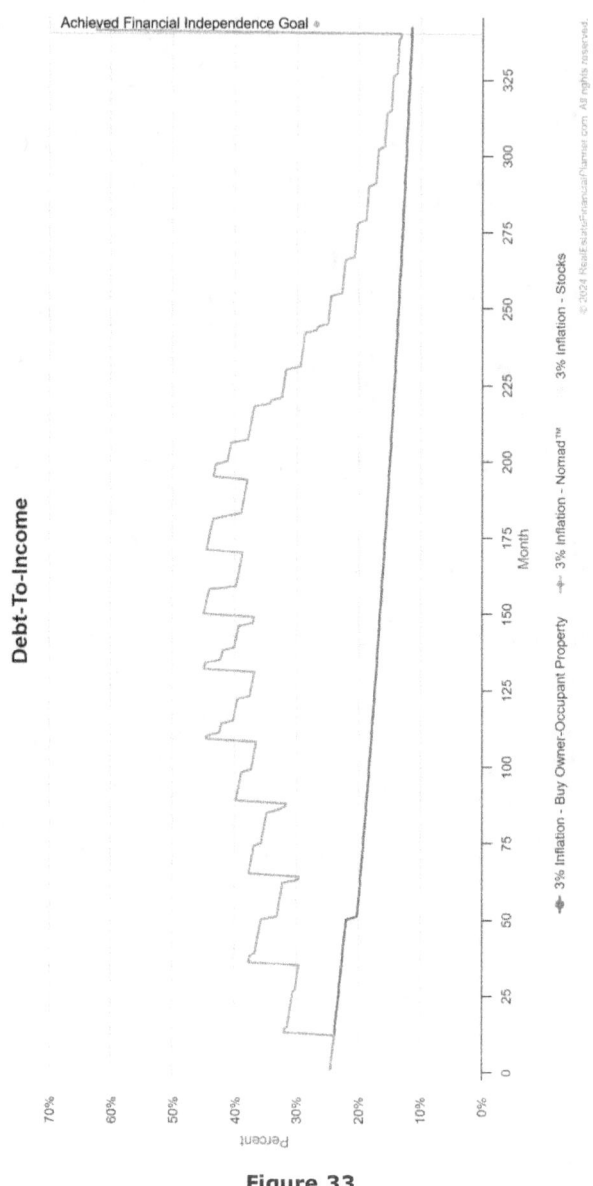

Figure 33

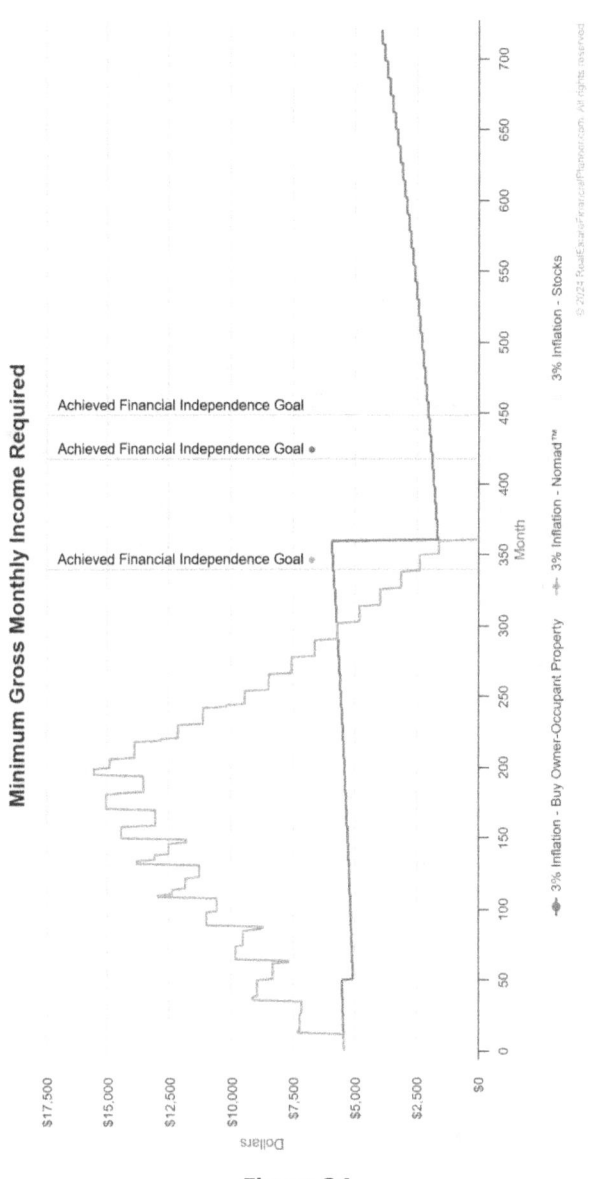

Figure 34

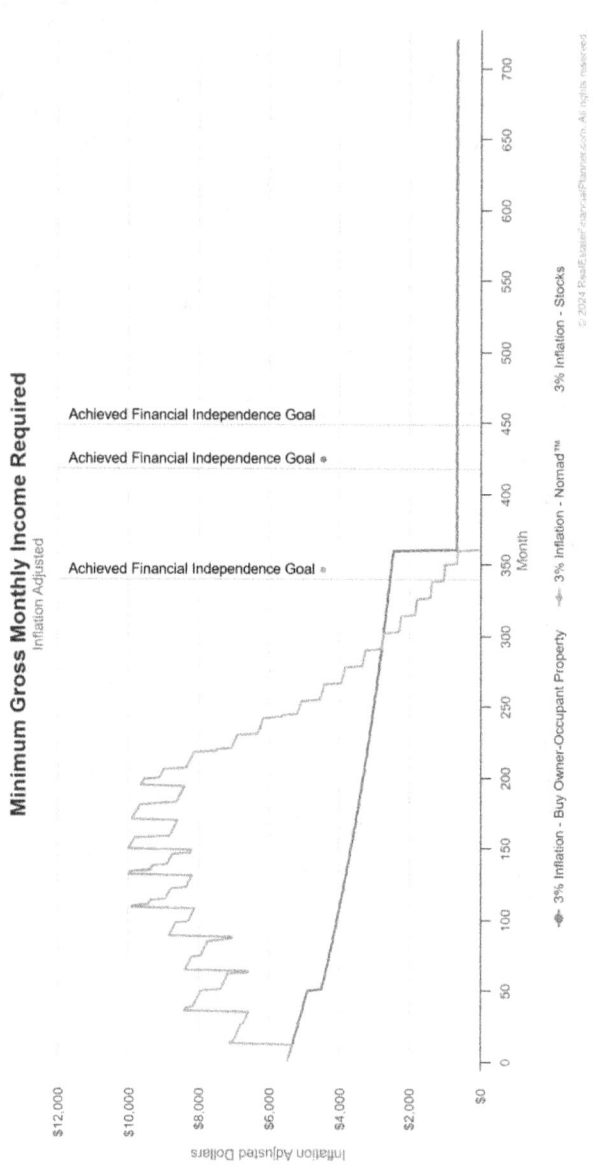

Figure 35

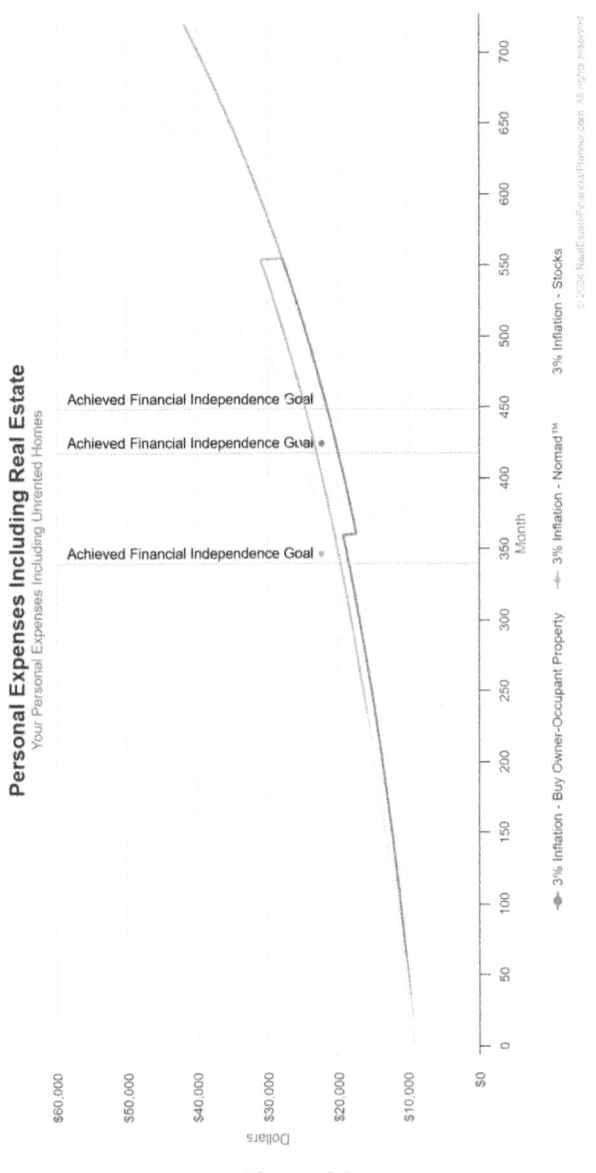

Figure 36

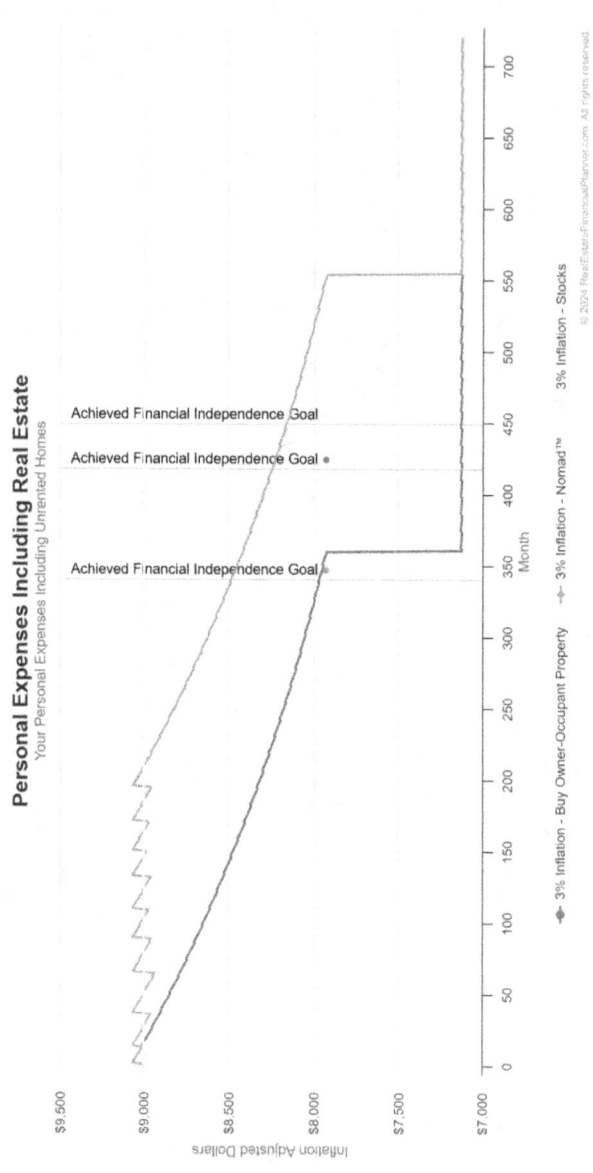

Figure 37

One of the reasons that buying a bunch of properties is better with inflation is that they take on a lot of long-term, fixed payment debt that they can pay off with future, inflated dollars. You can see this in **Figure 38**. They end up with about $3.25 million dollars in debt at the peak when Nomading™.

What is more interesting though is if we look at this adjusting for inflation back to today's dollars in **Figure 39**.

When they do that, they're taking on what feels more like $2 million in total mortgage debt in today's dollars.

With increased debt comes increased risk. And, we measure risk in several forms. One we already discussed—debt-to-income. You saw that their debt-to-income was much higher when they buy 10 Nomad™ properties. They're pushing the lender's limit as to what they will allow and still offer to finance.

Another measure of risk is their total debt compared to their net worth as shown in **Figure 40**. They do have close to twice this measure of risk compared to just buying the one owner-occupant property and this risk measurement remains elevated for years as they're actively acquiring properties.

A variation on this measure of risk is comparing how much debt they have to how much they have in liquid assets like cash, stocks and bonds—explicitly not equity in properties which is illiquid and harder to access. That's the chart in **Figure 41**.

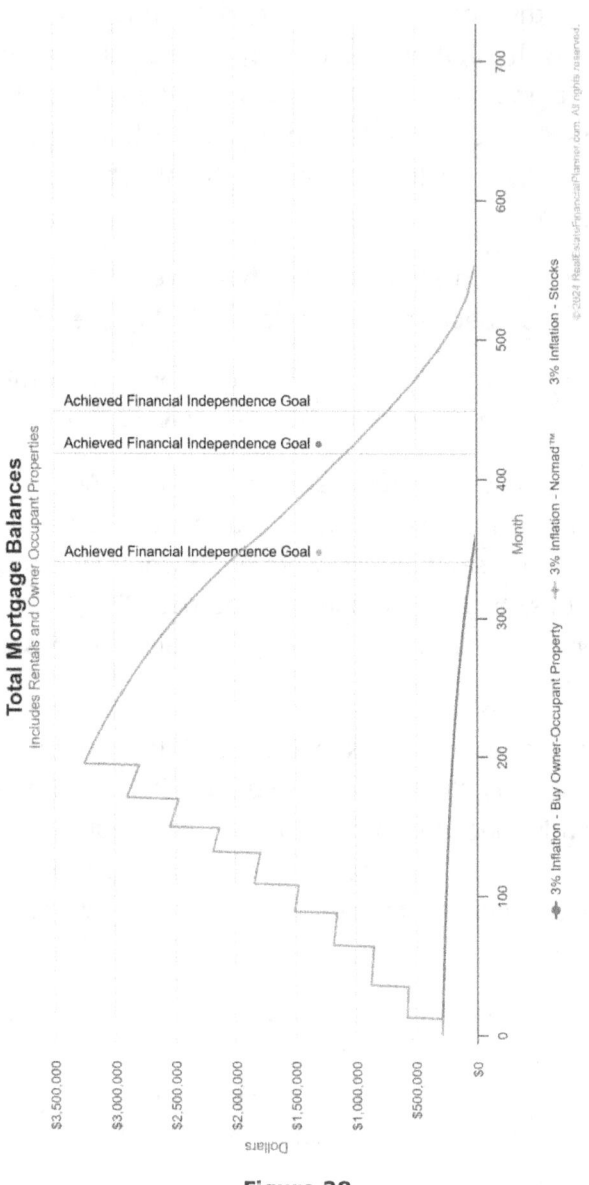

Figure 38

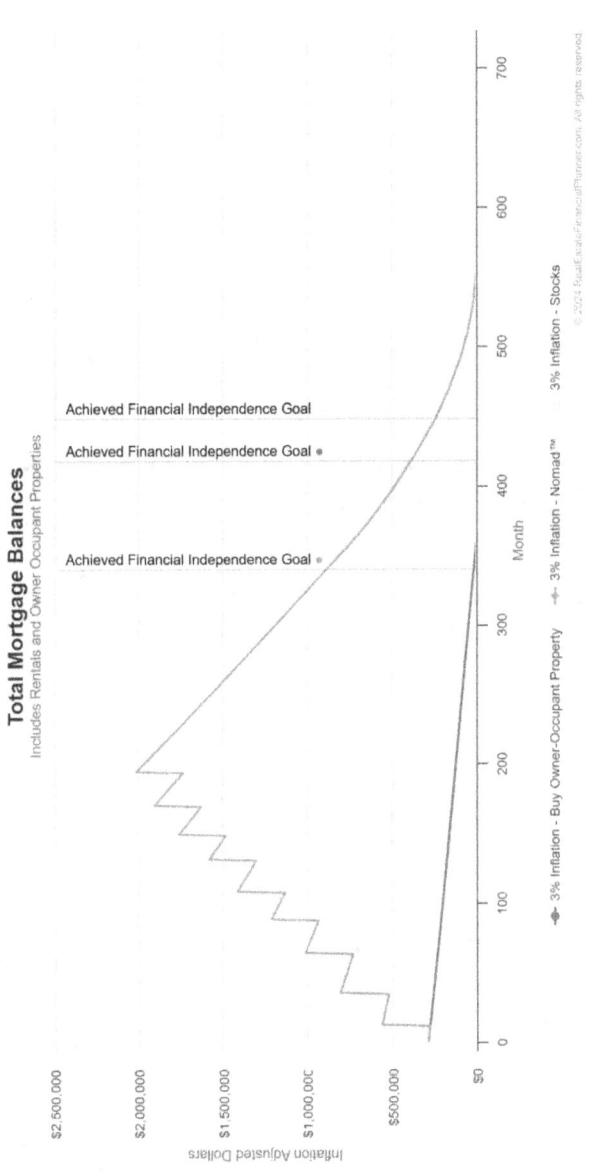

Figure 39

82

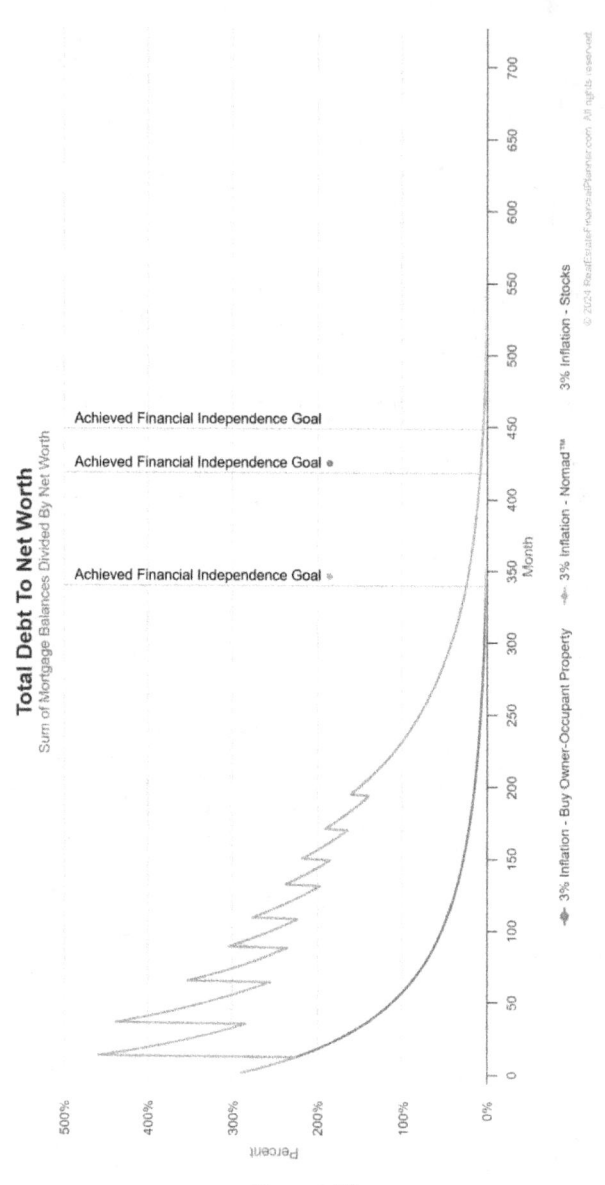

Figure 40

© 2024 James Orr. All rights reserved.

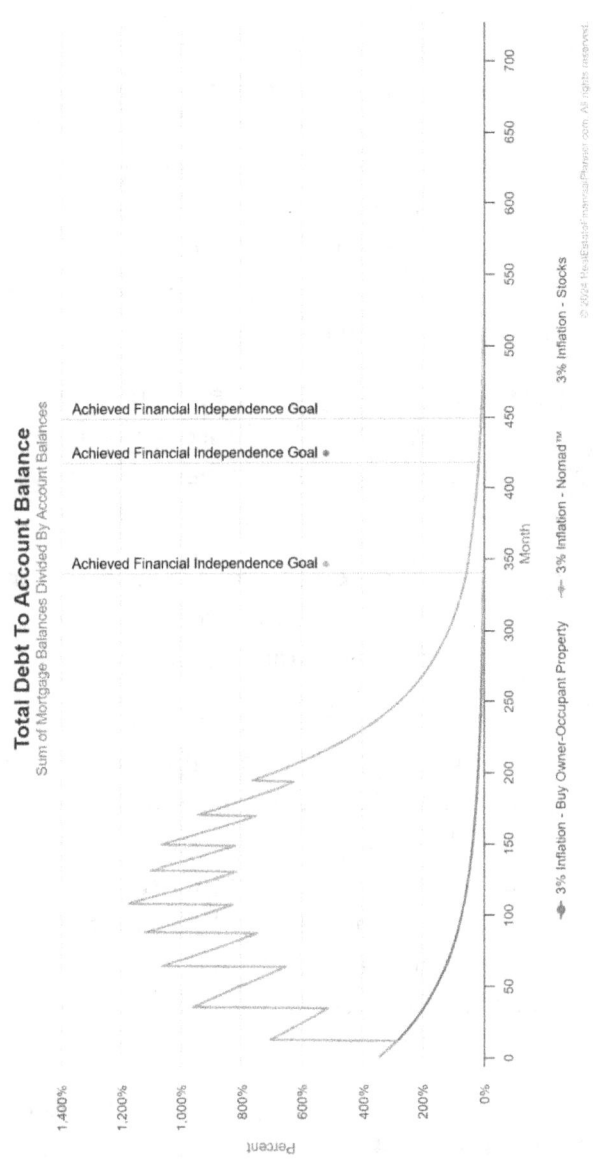

Figure 41

And you can see that this measure of risk shows significantly higher risk than the measure of debt to net worth. The max when they bought just an owner-occupant property was below 400%, but the max when they Nomad™ 10 times is almost 1,200% when they acquire property 6. Once they bought property 6 though their overall debt to account balance measure of risk has maxed out and is, overall, trending down except for the bumps up with each subsequent property purchase.

With each new property they buy, they take on responsibility for new mortgage payments. In **Figure 42**, you can see the mortgage payments on just the properties that are rentals (after they've lived there for a year).

They stairstep up to max out when the last property is purchased and then, 30 years after each purchase as mortgages are paid off, they stairstep back down.

As I've previously explained in detail, mortgage payments do not increase with inflation. In fact, if we adjust that same chart for inflation back to today's dollars, the payments on these 9 rental property mortgages seem to get cheaper the longer we hold them as shown in **Figure 43**. Such that, even at the peak of 9 rental properties, the max they ever feel like in today's dollars will be a little over $13,000 even though in inflated dollars, they're really over $20K per month.

But they all have rents coming in to help make those payments. In **Figure 44**, you can see that rents are inching up with both inflation and with each new conversion of the last Nomad™ property to a rental.

If we adjust back for inflation to today's dollars, you can see the bump from each new Nomad™ property becoming a rental, but the upward increase from inflation disappears. Eventually, rents seem to stabilize at just under $20,000 per month in today's dollars as seen in **Figure 45**.

There are other expenses besides mortgage like PMI, vacancy, taxes, insurance, maintenance and property management if they were not managing the properties themselves (which they are in our modeling). But, if we look at the rent minus all the expenses, we can see the cash flow that is being generated by these properties in **Figure 46**.

If we adjust cash flow for inflation back to today's dollars, **Figure 47**, you can see that cash flow maxes out at just under $15,000 per month. But, if you look early on, there is definitely negative cash flow.

If they had put more down—and not the 5% they did to buy each Nomad™ property as an owner-occupant, they would have had positive cash flow. So, really this negative cash flow is deferred down payment. It is paying monthly instead of putting more down up front to get rid of the negative cash flow.

These are $300,000 properties, so putting 5% down is approximately $15,000. If they put 25% down, they'd have a little positive cash flow. 20% is $60,000. So, they could have put $60,000 more down per property to not have negative cash flow.

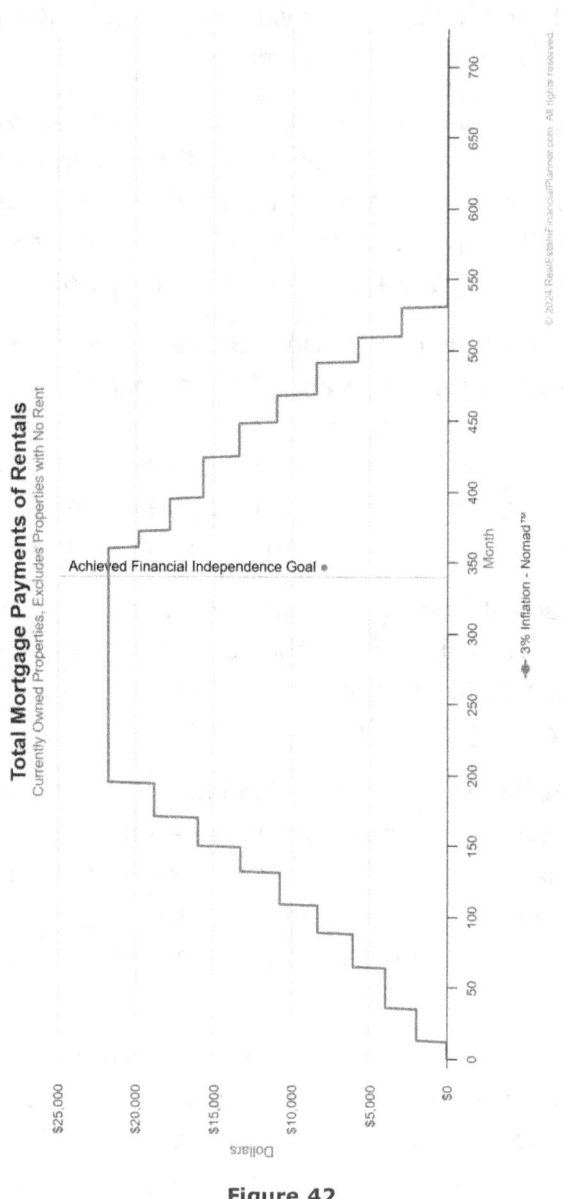

Figure 42

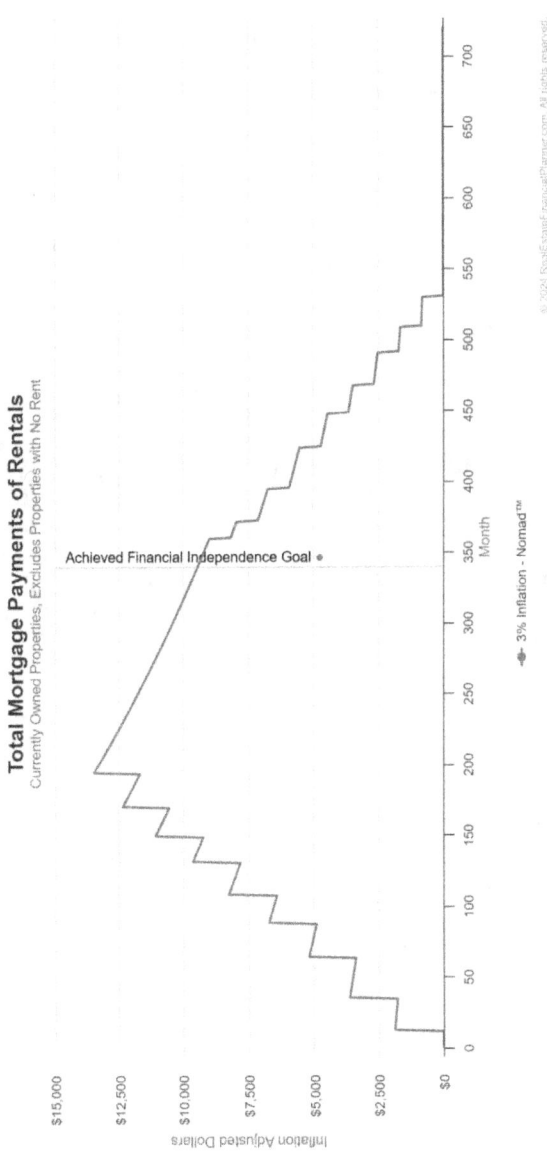

Figure 43

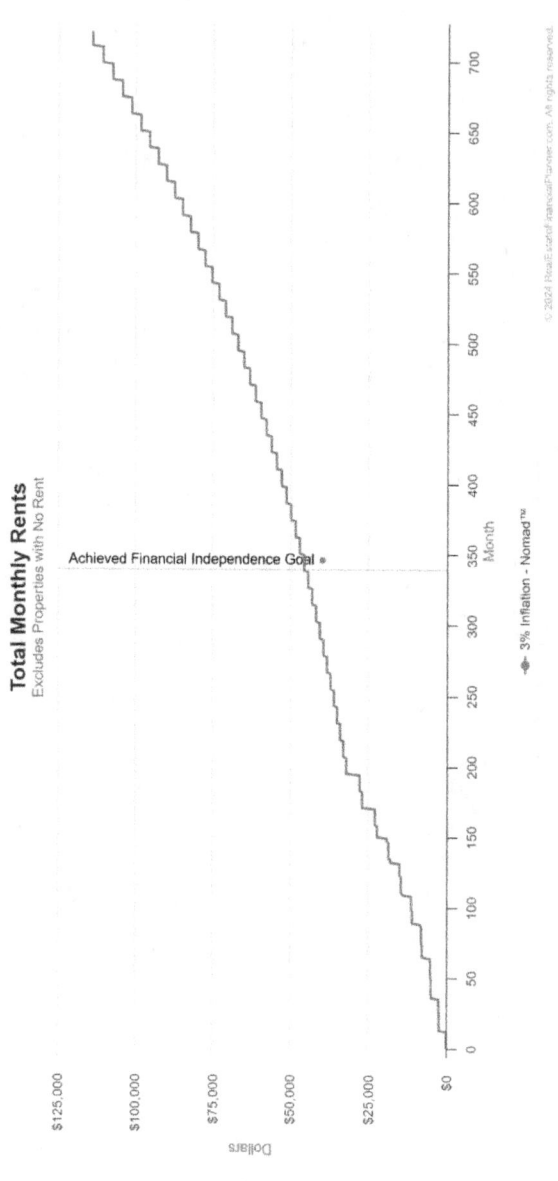

Figure 44

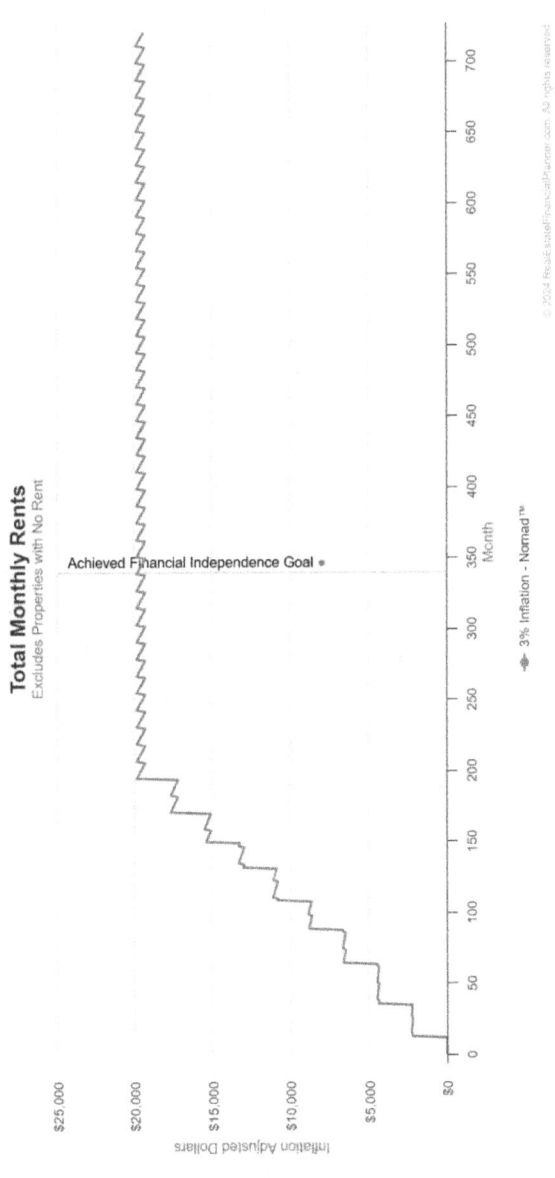

Figure 45

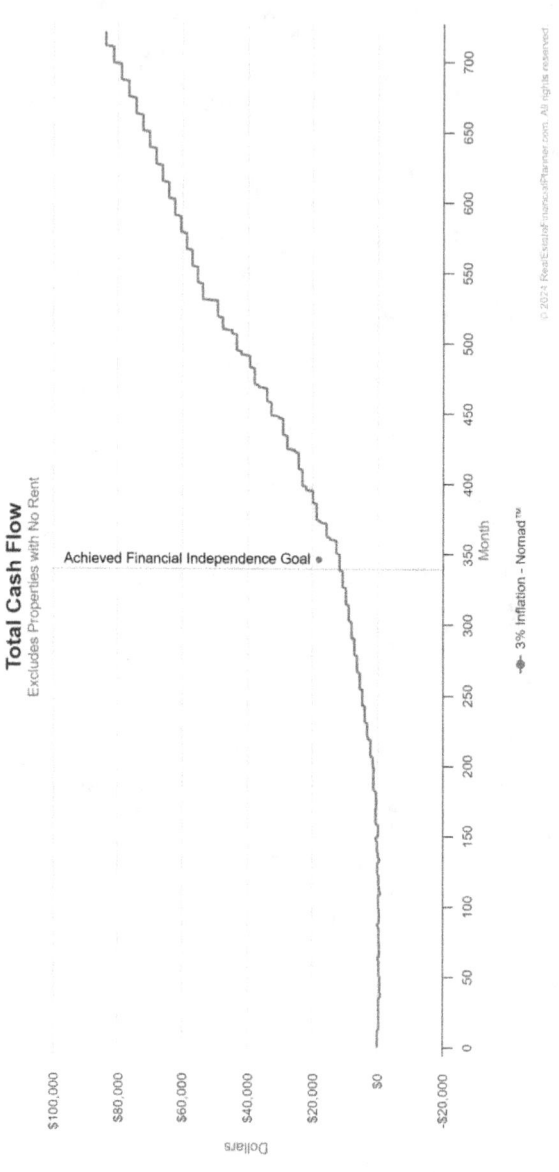

Figure 46

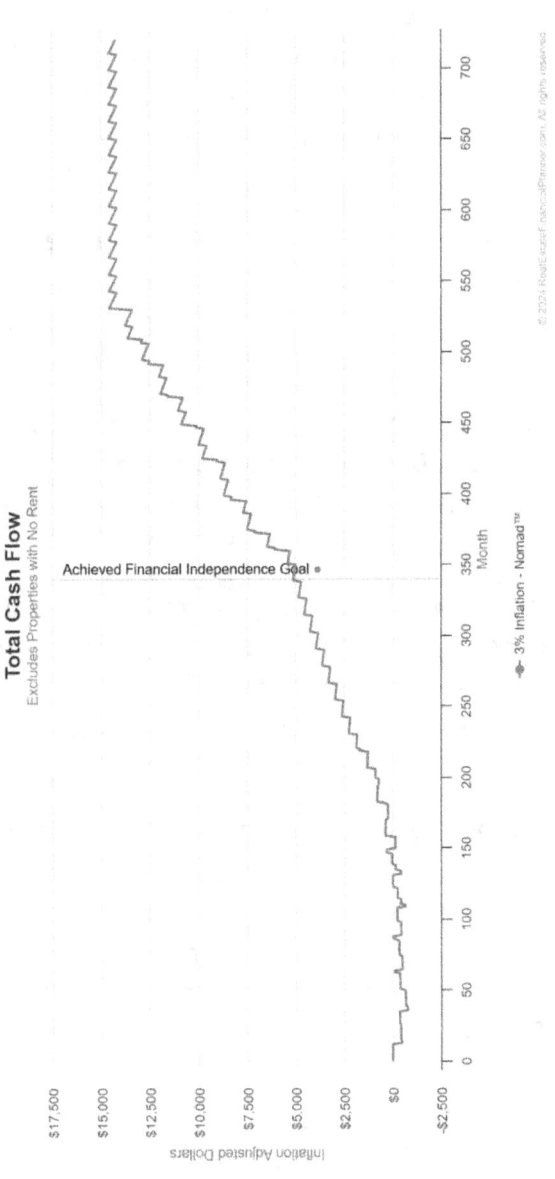

Figure 47

Or, they could choose to pay a little negative cash flow on the property from their savings each month and buy the property sooner to capture the other benefits like appreciation, debt paydown and the tax benefits of owning the property (*Cash Flow from Depreciation*™).

How much negative cash flow? It depends on the property. **Figure 48** shows the total amount of negative cash flow until rents increase enough that the property has positive cash flow.

So, for the very first property they bought, instead of putting down an extra $60,000 to get positive cash flow from the very beginning, they instead paid some negative cash flow each month until they put out $16,599.29.

But they're really not even putting out that amount because there are tax benefits from owning the rental property which show up as extra cash in your pocket from not having to spend that money on taxes. We call that *Cash Flow from Depreciation*™.

Cash Flow from Depreciation™ lasts for 27.5 years from when you buy the property and then the benefit stops as shown in **Figure 49**. The more expensive the property, the larger the *Cash Flow from Depreciation*™ benefit is monthly since it is based on the value of the property itself (excluding the value of the land).

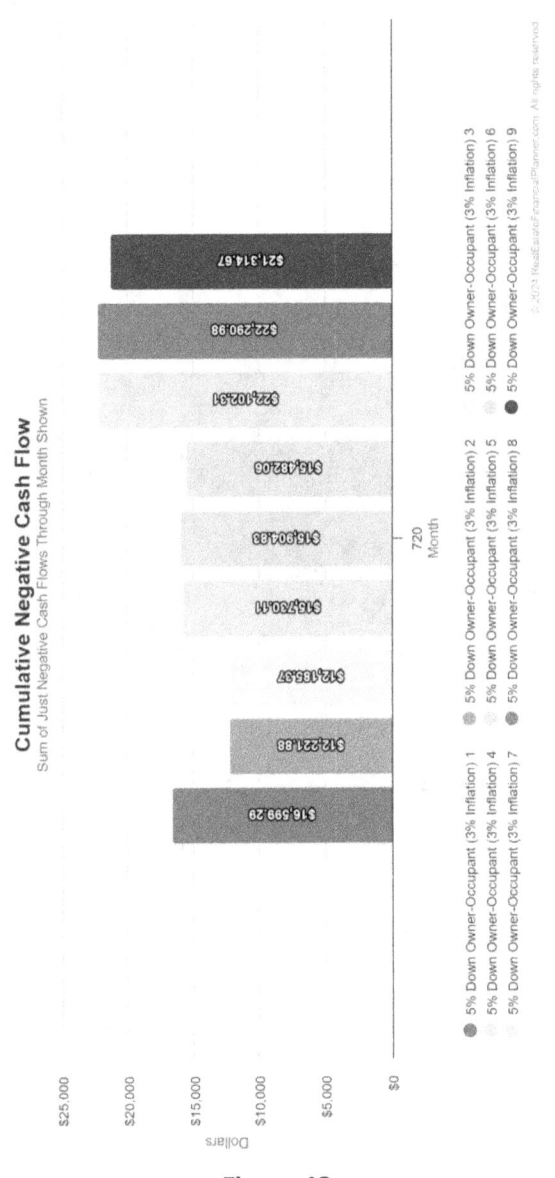

Figure 48

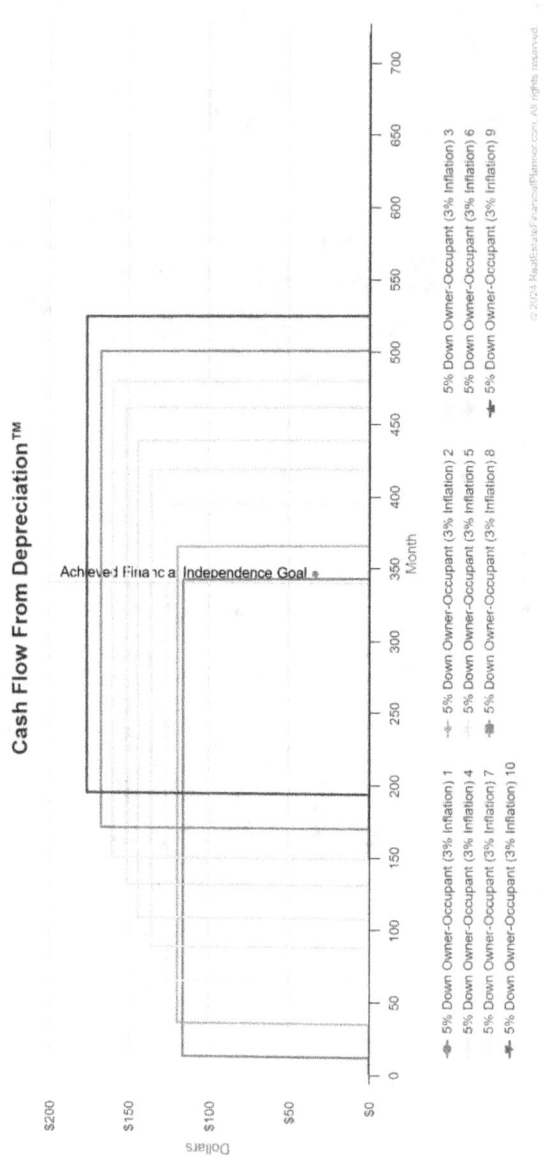

Figure 49

So, for the first property they buy, they're getting about $115.91 in *Cash Flow from Depreciation™* each month for the first 27.5 years it is a rental property. You see this in **Figure 50**.

What was -$495.52 in negative cash flow the first month it was a rental (month 13), really is -$379.61 when you include the *Cash Flow from Depreciation™*. When we combine cash flow with *Cash Flow from Depreciation™*, we call that *True Cash Flow™*.

If we look at the cumulative negative *True Cash Flow™* for each property over the entire period they had negative *True Cash Flow™*, you can see in **Figure 51** that it is much lower than the cumulative cash flow in **Figure 48**.

That means, for example with the first property they bought and converted to a rental, instead of putting almost $60,000 down, they really only needed to put $10,787.99 into the deal—and monthly with cheaper, inflated dollars—until they had positive *True Cash Flow™* on the property.

The total cumulative negative cash flow for all the properties combined was just under $154,000 as shown in **Figure 52**.

If we look at the total cumulative negative True Cash Flow™—which includes the offset from Cash Flow from Depreciation™—for all the properties combined it was just over $93,000 as shown in **Figure 53**.

Out of an abundance of clarity, this sums up all the negative cash or negative *True Cash Flow™* from each individual property even though the overall cash flow or *True Cash*

Flow™ when you look at all the properties combined might be positive.

For example, let's say you own 6 properties and 4 of them have great positive cash flow. But, the two most recent have negative cash flow. If you add up the cash flow from all 6, it is positive even with the two negative ones pulling the total down. For the charts of cumulative negative cash flow or *True Cash Flow*™, we still are counting the negative cash flows from properties 5 and 6.

I just gave you the total amount of cumulative negative cash flow and cumulative negative *True Cash Flow*™ but how much did they need to invest to acquire the properties with down payments and closing costs? In **Figure 54**, you can see that they had to invest a total of about $201K to acquire the 9 rentals as a Nomad™.

If we chart both the total amount invested and the cumulative negative cash flow on the same chart, **Figure 55**, you can see the relative sizes of the total down payment and closing costs to the cumulative negative cash flow they invested over time as well.

If we add these two together, we can now see the total amount invested including down payment, closing costs and negative cash flow in **Figure 56**. It works out to be just over $355K total for everything for all 9 rental properties as a Nomad™.

One of the benefits of inflation is that money spent later is worth less, so delaying down payments by accepting negative cash flow and paying it over time can be beneficial.

As we wind down the deep dive into the Nomad™ strategy at 3% inflation and before we compare it to other inflation environments with the same Nomad™ strategy, let's look at how asset allocation changes over time as they buy 10 properties—9 of them rentals. That's shown in **Figure 57**.

And, if you're familiar with my advanced asset allocation analysis, here's how that looks in **Figure 58**.

If we want to see the exact asset allocation for the month they achieve financial independence in month 340, it looks like **Figure 59**.

And their equity allocation for that same month looks like this in **Figure 60**.

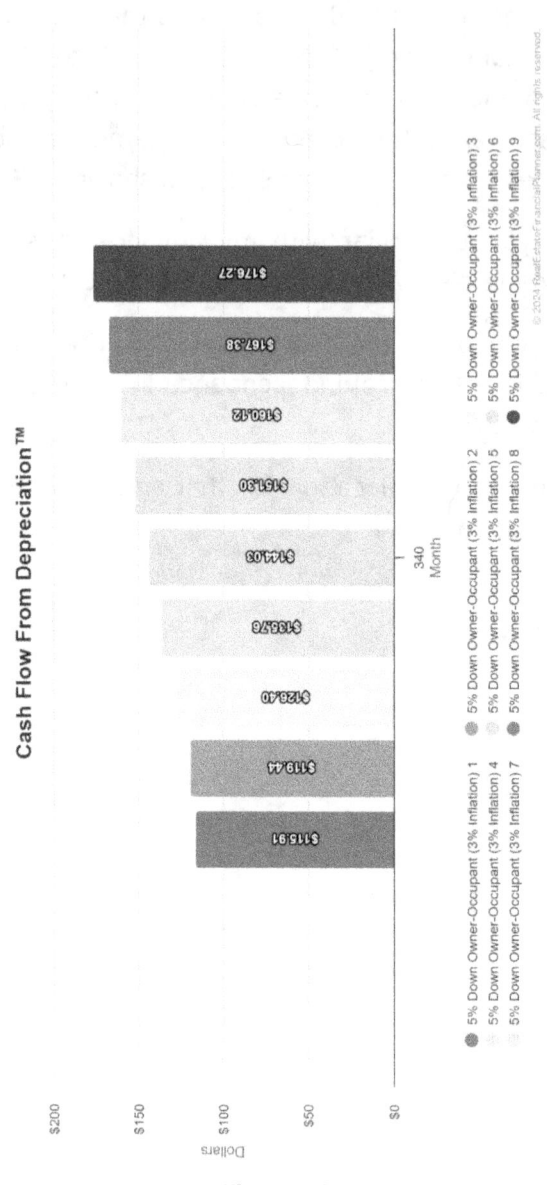

Figure 50

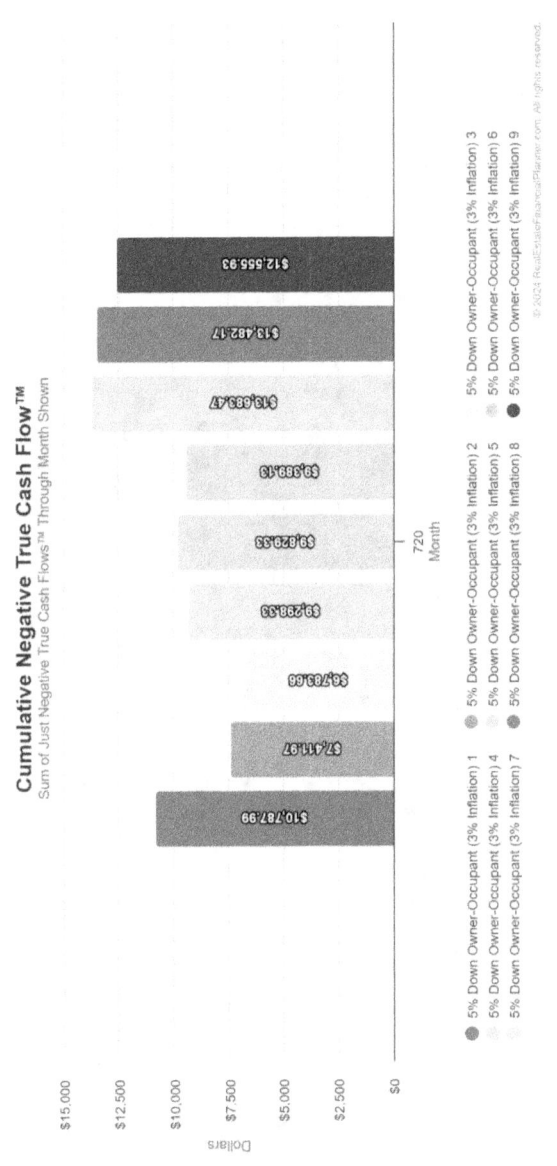

Figure 51

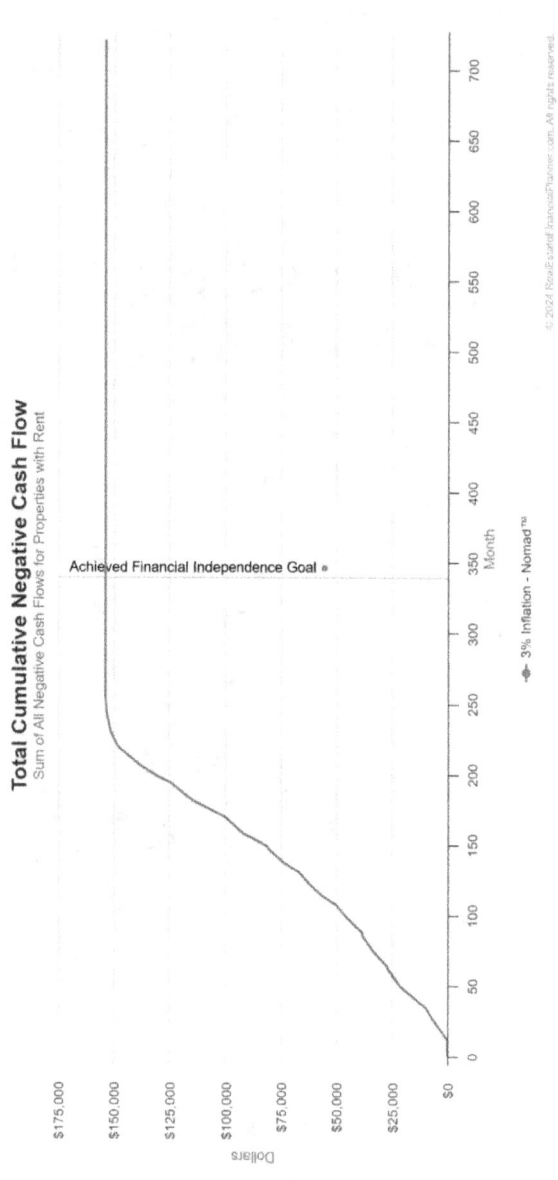

Figure 52

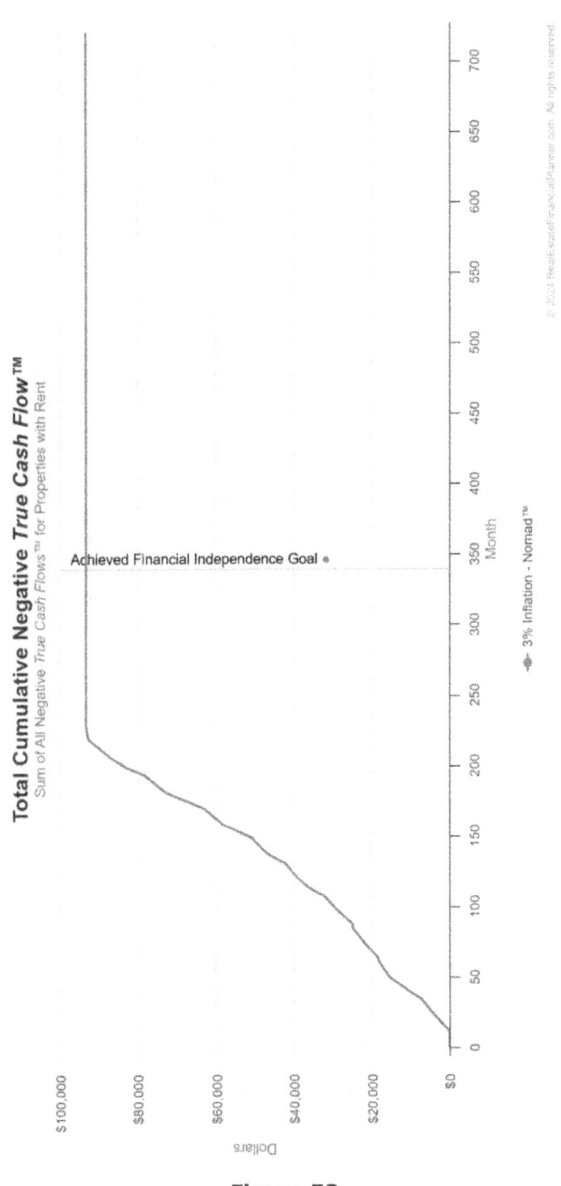

Figure 53

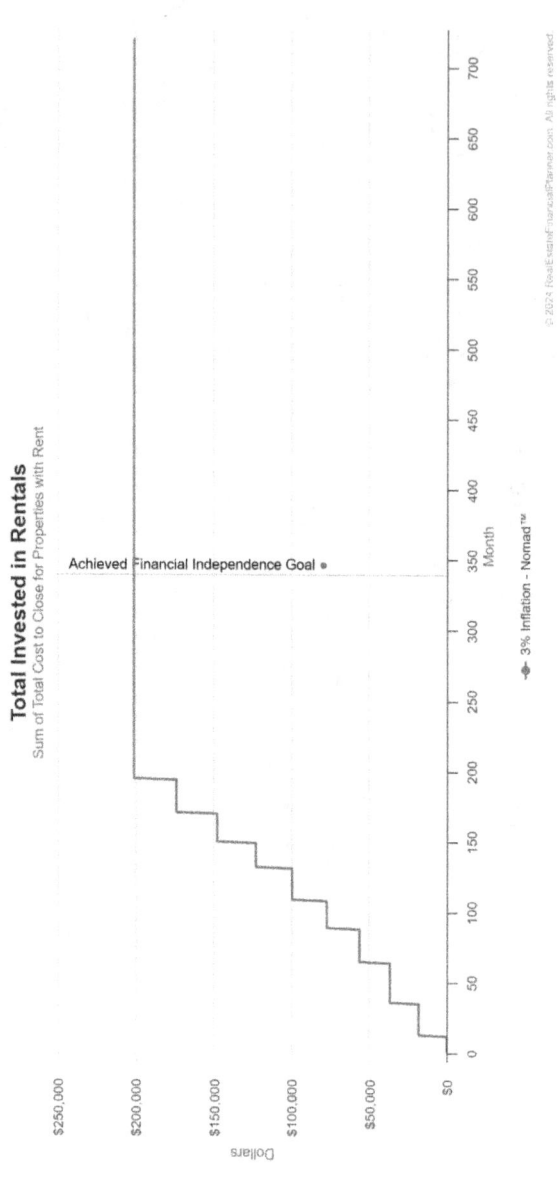

Figure 54

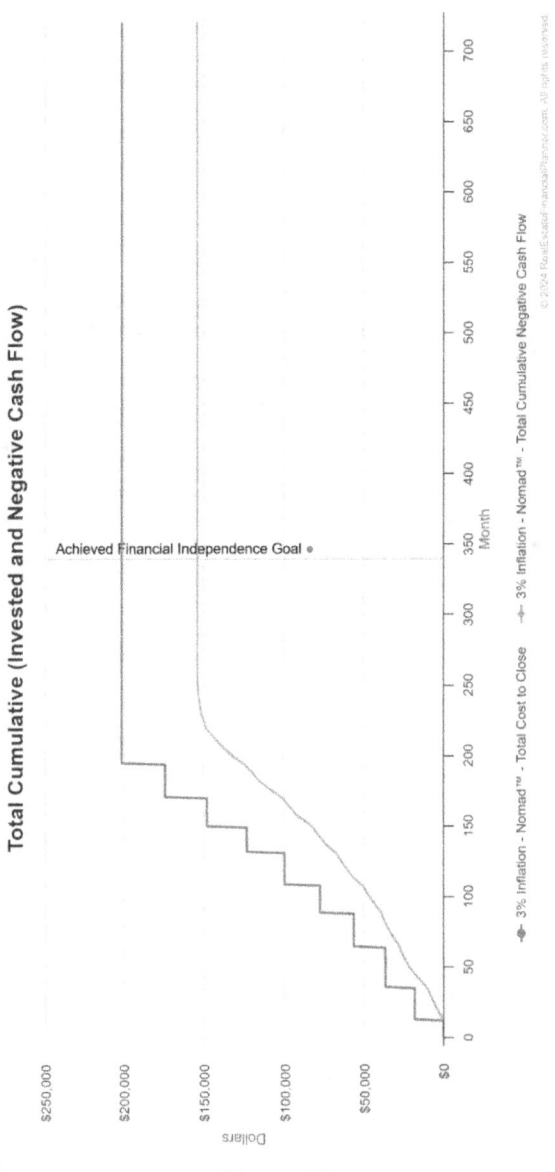

Figure 55

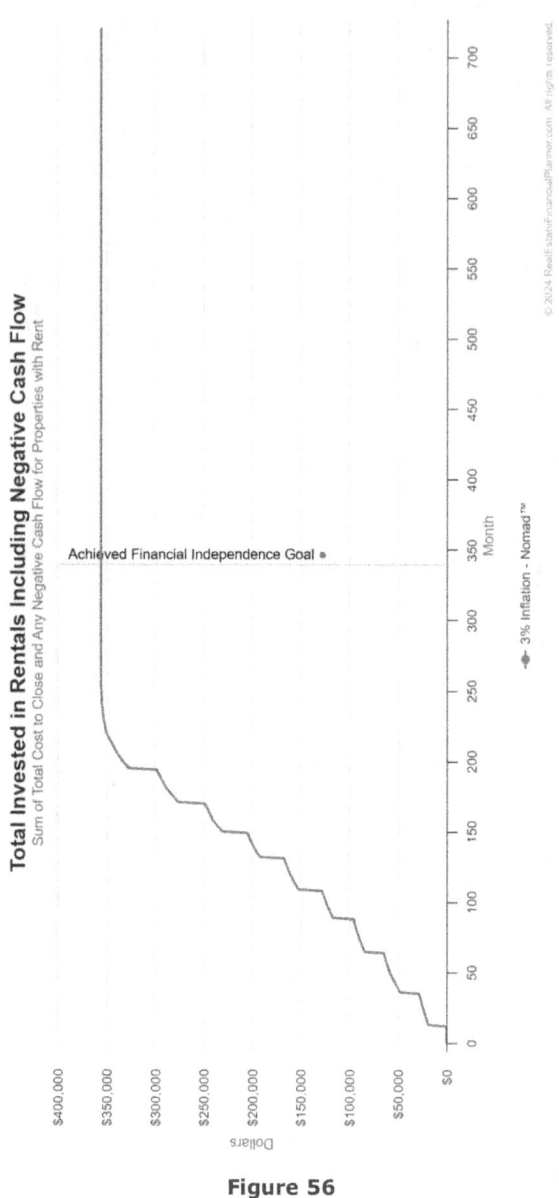

Figure 56

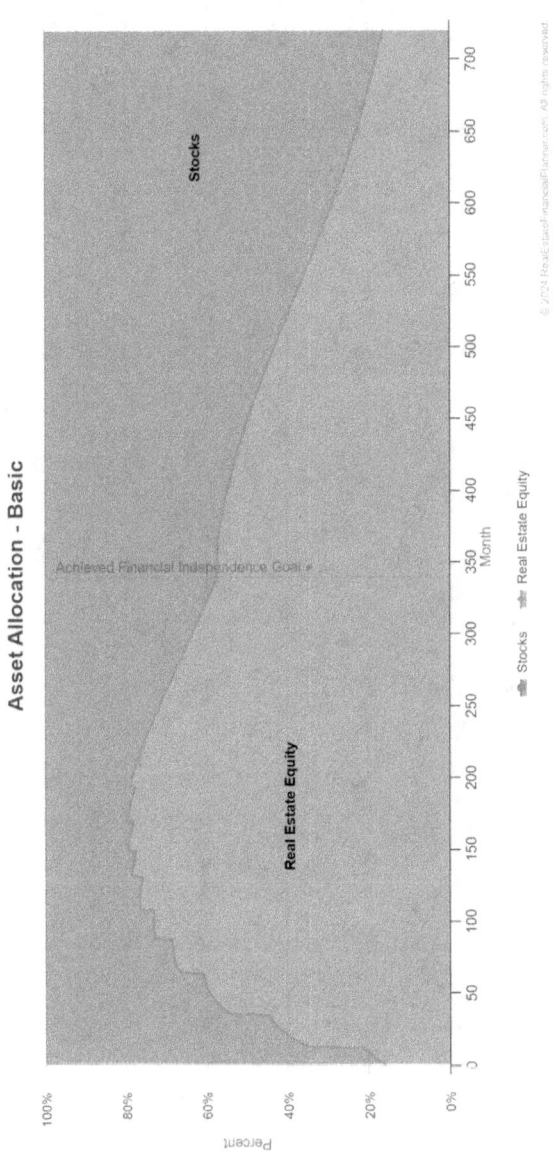

Figure 57

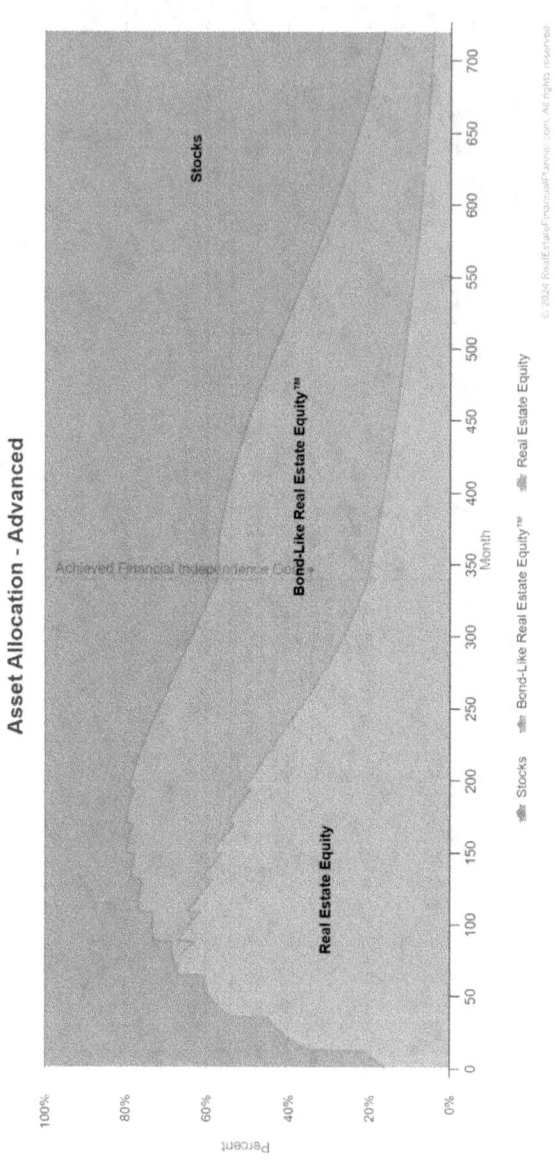

Figure 58

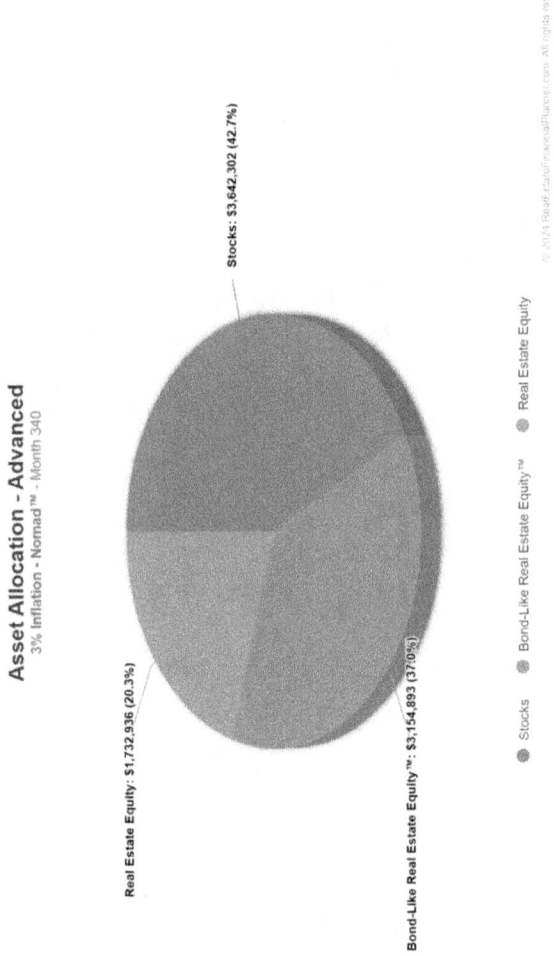

Asset Allocation - Advanced
3% Inflation - Nomad™ - Month 340

Stocks: $3,642,302 (42.7%)

Real Estate Equity: $1,732,936 (20.3%)

Bond-Like Real Estate Equity™: $3,154,893 (37.0%)

● Stocks   ● Bond-Like Real Estate Equity™   ● Real Estate Equity

Figure 59

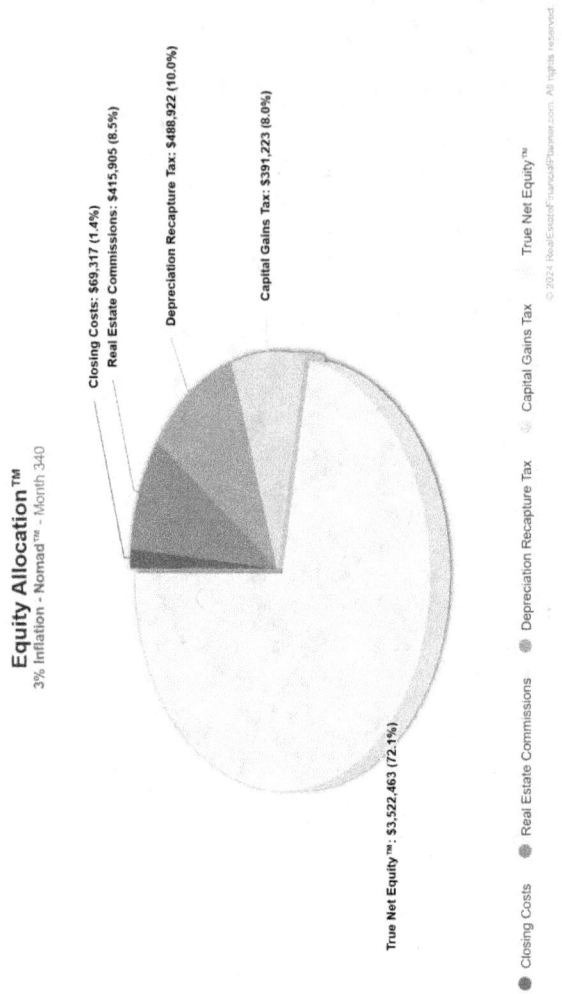

Equity Allocation™
3% Inflation - Nomad™ - Month 340

Closing Costs: $69,317 (1.4%)
Real Estate Commissions: $415,905 (8.5%)

Depreciation Recapture Tax: $488,922 (10.0%)

Capital Gains Tax: $391,223 (8.0%)

True Net Equity™: $3,522,463 (72.1%)

● Closing Costs ● Real Estate Commissions ● Depreciation Recapture Tax ● Capital Gains Tax True Net Equity™

© 2024 RealEstateFinancialPlanner.com. All rights reserved.

Figure 60

Nomad™ at Various Inflation Rates

Now that you have a much deeper understanding on the Nomad™ strategy and how it works at 3% inflation, let's look at how it performs with higher and lower inflation rates.

Figure 61 illustrates how long it takes to achieve financial independence using the Nomad™ strategy under different inflation scenarios.

Here's a breakdown of how the strategy performs at varying inflation levels and how it compares:

- 5% Inflation (Nomad™) vs. 4% Inflation (Nomad™)

    o *5% Inflation:* 21.42 years (257 months)
    o *4% Inflation:* 24.33 years (292 months)
    o *Difference:* The 5% inflation environment allows for financial independence 2.91 years (35 months) sooner than 4% inflation.

- 4% Inflation (Nomad™) vs. 3% Inflation (Nomad™)

    o *4% Inflation:* 24.33 years (292 months)
    o *3% Inflation:* 28.33 years (340 months)
    o *Difference:* Achieving financial independence occurs 4 years (48 months) sooner under 4% inflation compared to 3%.

- 3% Inflation (Nomad™) vs. 2% Inflation (Nomad™)

    o *3% Inflation:* 28.33 years (340 months)
    o *2% Inflation:* 31.17 years (374 months)

- *Difference:* With 3% inflation, financial independence is reached 2.84 years (34 months) sooner than at 2% inflation.

The Nomad™ strategy shows faster paths to financial independence as inflation increases, demonstrating its ability to leverage inflationary conditions through real estate investment and equity growth more effectively than other approaches.

As inflation increases, so does net worth while doing Nomad™ as well as shown in **Figure 62**.

However, if we adjust net worth for inflation back into today's dollars the strategy improves with inflation until they're financially independent. But that does not continue indefinitely after they stop working. All perform well and continue to grow in net worth, but some perform and grow faster than others. See **Figure 63**.

Before we model buying investment properties with 20% down payments after buying a single owner-occupant property in a variety of inflation environments, let's recap why real estate is often considered a hedge against inflation.

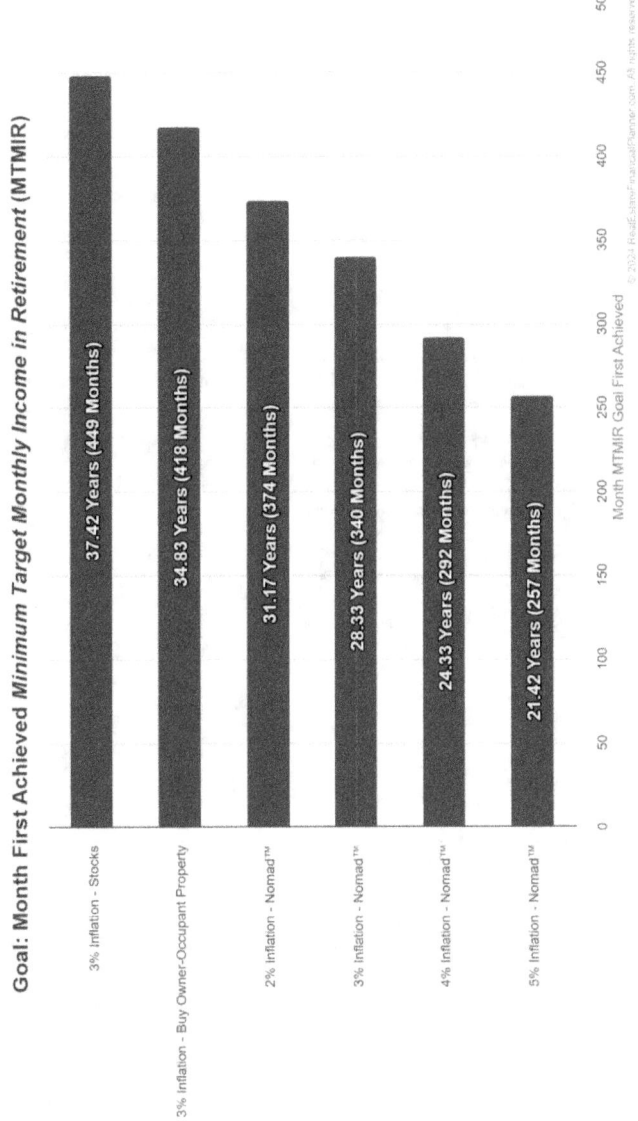

Figure 61

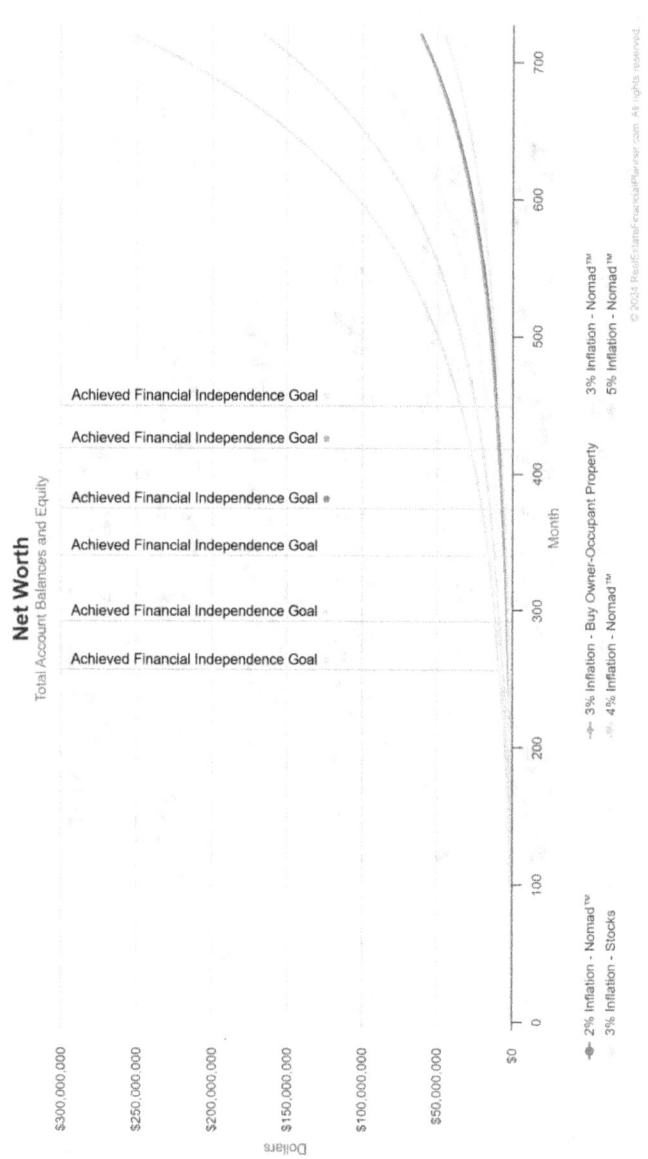

Figure 62

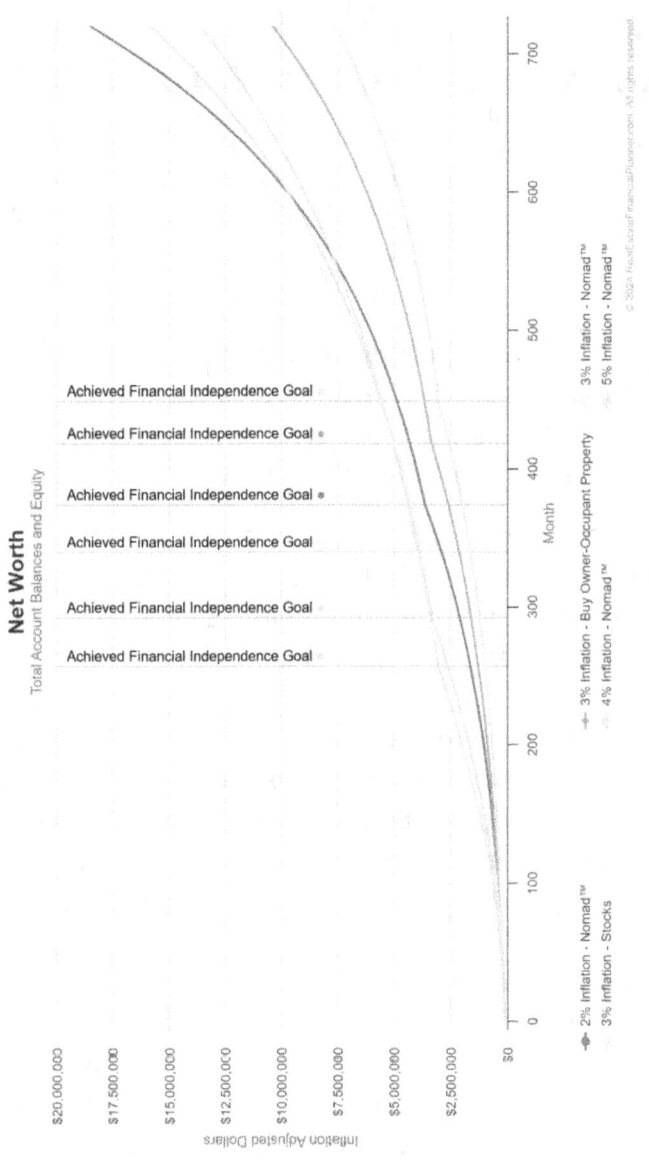

Figure 63

Why is Real Estate Considered a Hedge Against Inflation?

Real estate is often considered a strong hedge against inflation, making it an attractive asset class for investors looking to preserve and grow wealth over time.

Many of these ideas we've uncovered while we did our modeling, but to recap in one quick list here's why real estate is considered a hedge against inflation and often performs well in periods of high inflation:

- **Rent Increases** - Inflation often drives up rental income since rents typically rise in line with inflation. This provides property owners with additional cash flow, helping to offset rising costs and maintain or improve profitability.
- **Operating Expenses and Inflation** - While inflation raises costs for maintenance, property management, taxes, and insurance, these expenses usually represent a smaller portion of total rental property costs. Rent increases often cover or exceed these rising costs, preserving cash flow.
- **Fixed-Rate Mortgage Advantage** - Fixed-rate mortgages remain constant despite rising inflation, allowing owners to benefit from increasing property values and rents while their debt payments stay stable, effectively reducing the real cost of debt over time.

- **Property Appreciation** - Real estate typically appreciates over time, sometimes even slightly outpacing overall inflation. This appreciation increases equity, making your investments more valuable and helping preserve purchasing power.
- **Depreciating Value of Debt** - Inflation erodes the real value of debt, meaning future mortgage payments become cheaper in "real" terms. This allows you to pay off debt with money that has less purchasing power, reducing the burden of debt.
- **Tangible Asset** - As a tangible, physical asset, real estate retains intrinsic value, unlike cash, which loses purchasing power due to inflation. This makes real estate a more stable store of wealth.
- **Leverage Benefits** - Using leverage to acquire real estate can magnify returns during inflationary periods. As property values rise, your debt remains fixed, increasing your equity and maximizing gains.
- **Tax Benefits** - Real estate offers tax advantages, including depreciation, 1031 exchanges, and other incentives that help offset inflation-driven costs, preserving more of your wealth. More on this shortly.
- **Scarcity and Market Demand** - Real estate is often scarce in desirable markets. As demand for housing increases, prices and rents rise, providing a natural hedge against inflation and increasing the asset's worth.
- **Hedge Against Currency Depreciation** - Real estate helps protect against declining currency value by maintaining its worth relative to goods and services, offering a stable and inflation-resistant store of wealth. That's because real estate is primarily made up of goods

(construction materials) and services (construction related labor).

Buying 20% Rentals at Various Inflation Rates

Let's look at the models for buying 20% down payment rentals at various inflation rates.

In this model, we have them:

- Buy an owner-occupant property with 5% down payment just like we did with the homeowner.
- Then, buy up to 9 non-owner-occupant (investment) properties as rentals as soon as they save up enough down payments based on the same savings assumptions we previously discussed. They do not need to wait a year like they do with Nomad™, but they need to save up enough for the 20% down payment, closing costs and reserves for their personal expenses, this property, and all the previous properties they bought.

For all the real estate modeling, we're using the same property, but the financing does change when we switch from owner-occupant to investor. Investor loans have higher mortgage interest rates: 7.5% instead of 7.25% for owner-occupants including Nomads™.

Also, since they are putting at least 20% down they no longer have Private Mortgage Insurance (PMI). PMI is required if they put less than 20% down like they are doing with the owner-occupant properties—including Nomad™—

that they bought in our previous modeling. We included PMI when they put less than 20% down, but since they are putting more than 20% down now, we exclude it.

Because they now need to save up 20% down payments, closing costs and reserves it takes them longer to acquire the 9 rentals then it did when they were Nomading™.

For example, in **Figure 64**, you can see that it takes until month 222 to acquire all 10 properties when saving up 20% down. But, they were able to acquire 10 properties when Nomading™ in 195 months.

Now that you understand what the difference is between them buying an owner-occupant property then nine 20% down rentals and Nomading™, I won't keep you waiting to show you how this impacts their journey to financial independence.

In **Figure 65** you can see:

- **3% Inflation - Stocks** - This strategy takes the longest at 37.42 years (or 449 months) to reach financial independence. Investing purely in stocks without leveraging real estate results in slower progress compared to other real estate strategies.
- **3% Inflation - Buy Owner-Occupant Property** - Achieving financial independence by simply buying and living in an owner-occupied property takes 34.83 years (or 418 months), offering a modest improvement over stock investing.
- **2% Inflation - Buy Owner-Occupant Property + 9 Rentals** - This strategy accelerates the timeline

significantly, achieving financial independence in 31.50 years (or 378 months) due to the combination of leverage and rental income growth.

- **2% Inflation - Nomad™** - Similar to the 2% inflation rental approach, the Nomad™ strategy takes 31.17 years (or 374 months) to reach financial independence. Not much of an improvement to Nomad™ versus just buying 20% down payment rentals at 2% inflation.
- **3% Inflation - Buy Owner-Occupant Property + 9 Rentals** - With 3% inflation, this approach reaches financial independence in 29.33 years (or 352 months).
- **3% Inflation - Nomad™** - This strategy achieves financial independence in 28.33 years (or 340 months), outperforming the simple buy-and-hold rental strategy by a year due to more aggressive leveraging and strategic moves.
- **4% Inflation - Buy Owner-Occupant Property + 9 Rentals** - The higher inflation rate further accelerates financial independence to 27.17 years (or 326 months), illustrating the benefits of leveraging real estate during inflationary times.
- **5% Inflation - Buy Owner-Occupant Property + 9 Rentals** - This scenario takes 25.33 years (or 304 months) to reach financial independence, showing that higher inflation can work in favor of leveraged real estate investors.
- **4% Inflation - Nomad™** - With 4% inflation, the Nomad™ strategy achieves financial independence even faster at 24.33 years (or 292 months). This is significantly faster than even buying 20% down rentals as an investor. It seems that the higher the inflation is

the better Nomad™ is even compared to putting 20% down.

- **5% Inflation - Nomad™** - The fastest path to financial independence among the scenarios presented, taking only 21.42 years (or 257 months). This demonstrates how the Nomad™ strategy thrives in high inflation.

In summary, leveraging real estate, whether through a combination of owner-occupant and rental properties or by using the Nomad™ strategy, outpaces pure stock investments in building wealth and reaching financial independence faster, especially in higher inflationary environments.

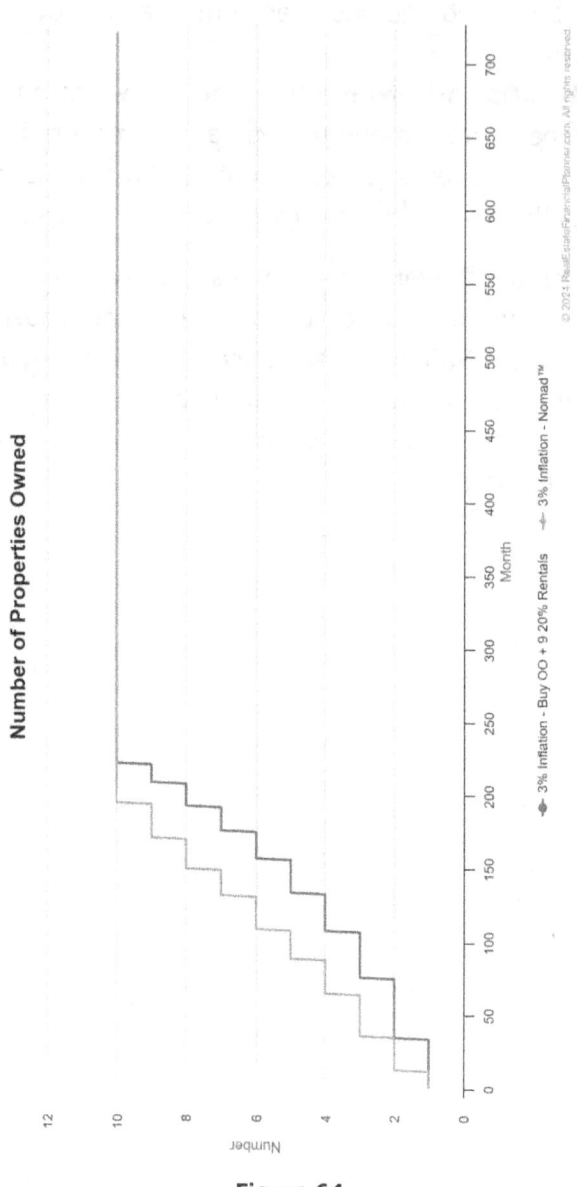

Figure 64

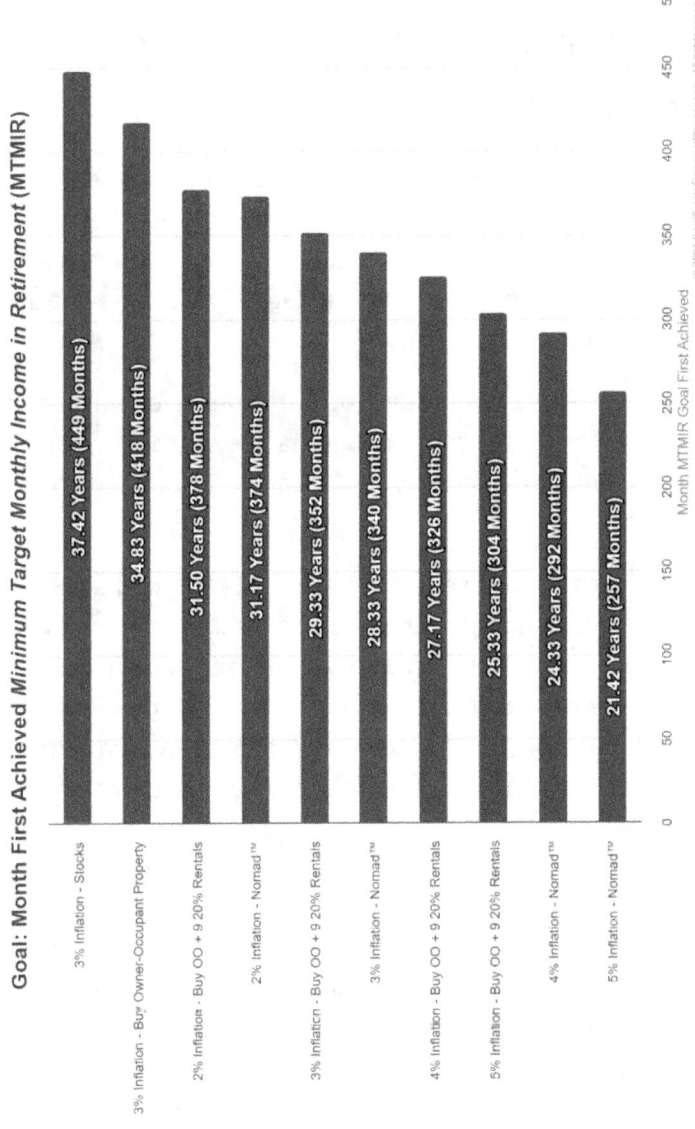

Figure 65

Tax Implications of High Inflation for Real Estate Investors

Higher inflation impacts the tax situation for real estate investors in various ways, presenting both challenges and opportunities. Here's a breakdown of the key implications you should consider as a real estate investor navigating a high-inflation environment:

This section is not intended to serve as a comprehensive guide on taxes, but it highlights key areas related to inflation. Always discuss your specific situation with a tax professional.

- **Accelerated Depreciation Benefits** - Using strategies like cost segregation or bonus depreciation allows you to accelerate depreciation and take larger deductions upfront when dollars have more purchasing power. This can be an effective tax strategy, especially in a high-inflation environment where the value of future dollars diminishes.
- **Higher Property Prices and Capital Gains** - When property values rise due to inflation, the potential capital gains from selling a property increase. This can result in a larger tax liability when you sell, as your gain is higher. However, remember that you're paying these taxes with "cheaper" dollars due to inflation, reducing the real impact of the tax liability over time.

- **Depreciation Basis and Inflation** - Depreciation is calculated based on the value of the property at the time of purchase. If you buy properties at higher prices during a high-inflation period, your annual depreciation deduction increases. This can offer a greater tax shelter for rental income in the short term, reducing taxable income. However, it's important to note that this depreciation is based on the purchase value, so when inflation drives up property values over time, depreciation remains based on the initial purchase price.
- **Inflation and 1031 Exchanges** - As inflation drives property values higher, the gains you'd realize on selling an appreciated property increase. Using a 1031 exchange (a mechanism allowing you to defer taxes when exchanging one property for another of like-kind) can help defer significant capital gains taxes, enabling you to reinvest in higher-value properties without an immediate tax hit.
- **Bracket Creep Due to Inflation** - Rising rental income or capital gains from property appreciation when selling can push you into higher tax brackets due to inflation. This "bracket creep" can increase the portion of your income subject to higher tax rates, even if your real income adjusted for inflation remains steady.
- **Tax Deductions on Higher Expenses** - Inflation increases expenses such as maintenance, property management, and insurance. While these higher costs can reduce cash flow, they also lead to larger tax-deductible expenses, potentially reducing taxable income and offsetting some of the impact of higher rental income due to inflation.

- **Property Taxes Rising with Inflation** - As property values rise due to inflation, property taxes often follow. While these taxes are deductible expenses for rental properties, they also represent an increasing cost to factor into your tax planning. Rising property taxes can reduce net cash flow but offer additional tax deductions.
- **Mortgage Interest Deduction Stability** - If you hold a fixed-rate mortgage, your interest payments remain stable despite inflation. While this offers stability, the real value of the deduction decreases as inflation erodes purchasing power. Still, it can provide consistent deductions even as your rental income rises.
- **Tax Benefits of Holding vs. Selling** - Holding a property during high inflation allows you to benefit from appreciation without realizing taxable gains. Selling, however, may trigger significant capital gains taxes on the appreciated value. Refinancing instead of selling can enable you to access equity while deferring taxes. Check out *Should I Sell My Rental Property?* and *Should I Refi My Rental Property?* in *The Real Estate Investing Mentor* series for more information on the calculations and considerations for selling and refinancing rental properties.
- **State Tax Implications** - State-level property taxes and regulations vary, and inflation may impact how your state reassesses and taxes properties. Be aware of local tax implications as they may differ significantly.
- **Inflation and Estate Taxes** - Higher property values due to inflation can push estates over federal or state estate tax exemption limits, increasing potential tax liabilities for heirs. Strategies such as gifting, setting up

trusts, or other estate planning tools can help mitigate this risk.

Inflation's impact on real estate taxes is complex, offering both opportunities for strategic tax planning and challenges due to increased costs and potential tax liabilities. Working closely with a tax professional can help you navigate these changes effectively and take advantage of the benefits while mitigating downsides.

House Hackers and Inflation

House hacking is a real estate strategy where you purchase a property, live in a portion of it, and rent out the remaining space to generate rental income. This could involve buying a multi-unit property and living in one unit while renting out the others, or living in a single-family home while renting out rooms to roommates. The goal is often to use the rental income to cover some—or all—of your housing expenses, creating an affordable path to homeownership and a way to build wealth through real estate.

House hackers experience many of the same benefits and challenges we've discussed throughout the inflation modeling for real estate investors. However, there are some specific ways that inflation impacts their unique strategy worth highlighting.

- **Increased Demand for Roommates** - During periods of high inflation, many renters find their finances stretched due to rising costs of living, including housing, utilities, and everyday essentials. This often drives more people to seek shared living arrangements to split costs and save money. As a house hacker renting out portions of your property, this increased demand for roommates can make it easier to find tenants and potentially raise rents to market rates, boosting your overall rental income.

- **Rising Rental Income** - Inflation tends to drive up rental prices, meaning house hackers can benefit by charging higher rent for rooms or units within their property. This helps offset increased costs from inflation, such as maintenance, insurance and property taxes, and can lead to improved cash flow. Unlike traditional homeowners who bear all costs themselves, house hackers can cover a portion—or even all—of their mortgage and expenses through rent.

- **Fixed-Rate Mortgage Stability** - Similar to other real estate investors, house hackers with a fixed-rate mortgage are shielded from rising housing costs driven by inflation. While their mortgage payment remains stable, the rents they collect can increase, improving their profit margins over time.

- **Operating Costs Increasing with Inflation** - House hackers are not immune to rising expenses such as maintenance, insurance, and property taxes, all of which can increase with inflation. However, these costs are often a smaller proportion of their total income, and the ability to adjust rents can help offset these increases.

- **Hedging Against Rising Rent Costs** - By owning their home and renting out portions of it, house hackers protect themselves from the rising costs of rent that impact traditional renters. This provides stability and predictability in their housing costs while they continue to benefit from market rent increases paid by tenants.

- **Property Value Appreciation** - Inflation often drives property values up, and house hackers benefit from the appreciation of their property's value. This increased equity can open up opportunities to access funds through refinancing or selling, enhancing their long-term wealth-building potential.
- **Tax Benefits** - House hackers may benefit from tax advantages, including depreciation on the rental portion of their property and deductions for operating expenses, which can further enhance their financial returns during periods of inflation.

In summary, house hacking can be a powerful strategy for mitigating the effects of inflation, providing stability in housing costs, and generating additional income to offset rising expenses. As inflation impacts renters and housing costs increase, house hackers are often well-positioned to benefit from increased demand for affordable, shared housing solutions.

Inflation Increases the Chasm Between the Haves and Have Nots

Inflation can create a significant gap between those who own assets ("the haves") and those who don't ("the have nots").

This happens because inflation tends to benefit asset owners while leaving non-owners scrambling to keep up with rising costs. If you want to protect and grow your wealth, buying assets—especially real estate—should be a priority.

Here's why it matters and why stretching to acquire at least an owner-occupant property is crucial, even if it seems challenging.

- **Asset Appreciation** - When inflation rises, assets like real estate and stocks tend to appreciate. This benefits people who own them, as their wealth grows with increasing equity leading to improved net worth. On the flip side, if you don't own assets, you miss out on this wealth-building opportunity and find yourself falling further behind. Buying your first owner-occupant property, even if you have to stretch to do it, gives you a foothold in this upward trend. Once you own an asset, you are positioned to benefit every time inflation raises market values. Then, ideally, repeat this process to gain a larger foothold with each acquisition.
- **Rising Rent Costs** - If you're a renter, inflation hits hard. Rent prices almost always increase over time, eroding your purchasing power and making it difficult to save or invest. In contrast, landlords and property owners benefit from these rising rents, building wealth as their rental income climbs. You will want to be on the right side of this market dynamic. That's why buying your own place—maybe even one where you can house hack and rent out portions of it—is a game changer. It stops you from being on the losing end of rising rents and can even turn rent inflation into a wealth-building tool.

- **Fixed Debt Payments** - When you buy a property with a fixed-rate mortgage, inflation becomes your ally. Your debt payments remain unchanged even as the value of money erodes, effectively reducing the real cost of your debt. This gives you a massive advantage over time. If you can stretch to buy that first property, you lock in this protection and can leverage it further by acquiring more properties using strategies like Nomading™, where you put a small amount down, move into a new home, and keep the previous one as a rental. Each property you acquire with fixed debt becomes an inflation shield.
- **Wage Growth Lag** - Inflation can drive up wages, but often there is a lag or delay. If you rely solely on your income, you may find it difficult to keep pace. But if you own assets—especially cash-flowing ones like rental properties—you have another source of income that rises along with inflation. Owning assets isn't just about building wealth; it's about protecting your purchasing power. Stretch to buy assets now, even if it means tightening your budget temporarily. The alternative is a constant struggle to keep up.
- **Cost of Living Increases** - Inflation makes everything more expensive. Without assets, you'll likely spend more of your income just to cover basic needs, making it harder to save or invest. Real estate owners, on the other hand, benefit from rising property values and rental income, giving them the means to cover rising expenses. Owning assets changes the game. If you can't buy multiple properties right away, start by stretching to buy your own place or a small multifamily home that

you can live in and rent out. Every asset you own acts as a hedge against inflation.

- **Access to Investment Opportunities** - Inflation often creates opportunities to buy appreciating assets like real estate. But if you don't have the means to invest, you're stuck watching from the sidelines. If you can stretch to acquire at least $100,000 in assets—perhaps by using a Nomad™ strategy where you repeatedly buy owner-occupied properties with minimal down payments and keep them as rentals—you'll be better positioned to seize opportunities. Owning assets opens doors. Without them, you're left vulnerable to inflation's impact.
- **Inflation-Protected Investments** - Asset owners can invest in real estate, which tends to hold value during inflationary periods. Owning rental properties, for example, can generate cash flow that rises with inflation, offsetting your increased living costs. Real estate offers a tangible way to protect and grow your wealth. If you don't already own assets, now is the time to stretch and acquire them. Buying your own home is a great first step, and using leverage to acquire more assets magnifies your gains as inflation rises.

In summary, inflation rewards those with assets and punishes those without.

If you want to thrive during inflation, you need to prioritize buying assets—especially real estate. Even if it means stretching your finances, purchasing your first owner-occupant property and aiming to build at least $100,000 in assets can change your financial trajectory.

Use strategies like Nomading™ to acquire more assets with minimal upfront investment. The goal is to protect and grow your wealth, turning inflation into a force that works for you, not against you.

Asset Protection and Inflation

Inflation doesn't just affect your day-to-day expenses; it can also have a significant impact on the value of your assets and the strategies you use to protect them. If you want to shield yourself from unexpected costs, legal risks, or financial losses, understanding how inflation impacts asset protection is crucial. Here's what you need to consider:

- **Regular Asset Valuation and Insurance Coverage Adjustments** - High inflation can rapidly increase the value of your real estate and other assets, necessitating regular valuations to ensure your insurance coverage remains adequate. This process helps you avoid the risk of being underinsured as market values rise. Adjusting your insurance coverage is crucial to reflect these changes, covering both liability insurance—which protects against legal claims—and property insurance, which safeguards against damage or replacement costs. Inflation not only impacts the cost to rebuild, repair, or replace your property but also increases the potential costs of liability claims. Medical care, legal fees, and compensation related to accidents or incidents can all rise during high-inflation periods, increasing the need for sufficient liability coverage. As a result, you may need to consider more aggressive coverage adjustments and ensure your policies adequately reflect these rising risks. Periodically reassessing your insurance and overall asset protection strategies is a key component of maintaining security in a high-inflation environment.

- **Umbrella Insurance** - In a high inflation environment, the value of large claims can increase significantly, making it essential to have adequate umbrella insurance coverage. If you previously had $4 million in umbrella liability insurance, for example, that amount may no longer provide the same level of protection as it once did. Inflation erodes the value of this coverage, so consider increasing it to ensure you're adequately protected in the event of a major liability claim.

- **Legal Structures for Asset Protection** - While legal structures like limited liability companies (LLCs) or trusts play a vital role in safeguarding your assets from lawsuits, creditors, or other risks, their importance remains steady regardless of inflation. LLCs, for example, offer liability protection by separating personal assets from business or real estate investments, while trusts can shield assets and dictate their management and transfer. Even though inflation may lead to an increase in the value of your real estate holdings or other assets, the role and function of these legal structures do not fundamentally change. They remain essential tools for protecting your wealth and minimizing exposure to legal risks, regardless of inflationary pressures.

- **Cost to Defend Legal Claims** - While this is essentially part of your reserves, it underscores why aiming for 12 months or more of reserves per property, rather than a fixed amount or just six months per property, is critical. Inflation can drive up the cost of defending against legal claims or lawsuits, with rising legal fees, court costs, and potential settlements. Ideally, you may never need these reserves, but in the event that you do, having adequate funds can mean the difference between keeping all your properties and losing them. Strengthening your legal defense fund and ensuring access to strong legal counsel is a key component of comprehensive asset protection planning.

In summary, protecting your assets in a high-inflation environment demands a proactive approach. Regularly update your insurance coverage to reflect rising property values, consider increasing umbrella liability coverage to maintain adequate protection against escalating liability costs, and leverage legal structures such as LLCs and trusts to shield your rapidly appreciating assets. Inflation alters the asset protection landscape by driving up both values and associated costs; don't be caught off guard by being underinsured or inadequately protected. Proactively managing these risks can help preserve your wealth and ensure long-term financial security.

Asset Allocation and Inflation

Inflation can significantly impact the balance of your investment portfolio, including how your assets are allocated. For real estate investors, understanding and managing this impact is important for maintaining a diversified and effective strategy.

While some real estate investors focus solely on real estate and are dismissive of other asset classes, many of us recognize the value of a more balanced and nuanced approach to asset allocation.

- **Real Estate Growth Versus Other Investments** - During periods of high inflation, real estate portfolios often grow faster than other investments like stocks and bonds. This is due to inflation's influence on property values, rental income, and therefore cash flow, which can lead to faster wealth accumulation. In contrast, the stock market and related assets may continue performing at historical levels, often without a direct correlation to inflation. As a result, the value of your real estate investments may outpace other assets, causing shifts in your overall asset allocation.
- **Unexpected Portfolio Imbalances** - When real estate assets grow disproportionately due to inflation, you may find yourself with a higher concentration of your wealth tied up in real estate than originally planned. This imbalance can expose you to risks associated with lack of diversification and liquidity. It's essential to periodically reassess your portfolio to ensure it aligns with your long-term goals and risk tolerance, even as certain assets outperform others due to inflation.
- **Regular Asset Allocation Reviews** - High inflation can cause rapid changes in asset values, making it important to evaluate and potentially rebalance your portfolio more

frequently. Adjustments may involve increasing investments in underweighted asset classes, such as stocks, bonds, cash to maintain a diversified portfolio that meets your preferred asset allocation strategy. This proactive approach helps mitigate risks and ensures that your wealth is not overly concentrated in any one asset class, even during periods of rapid growth in real estate.

Leveraging 1031 Exchanges During Inflation

A 1031 exchange, named after Section 1031 of the Internal Revenue Code, allows real estate investors to defer capital gains taxes by reinvesting the proceeds from a sold property into a "like-kind" property.

During periods of high inflation, this strategy can become even more valuable as property values rise at an accelerated pace.

Here's how you can leverage 1031 exchanges to enhance your real estate returns in an inflationary environment:

- **Rising Property Values and Tax Deferral** - Inflation often drives up real estate prices, leading to significant appreciation of your property's value. When you sell a highly appreciated property, you could be subject to substantial capital gains taxes, eroding a large portion of your profits. However, by using a 1031 exchange, you can defer paying these taxes by reinvesting the proceeds into another like-kind property. This allows you to preserve more of your wealth and leverage the full value of your investment gains to acquire a higher-value property, maximizing your purchasing power in a rising market.

- **Maximizing Leverage in an Inflationary Market** - In an inflationary environment, leveraging your assets can be a strategic move. By using a 1031 exchange to upgrade to a more valuable or higher-performing property, you can amplify the benefits of rising rents, increased cash flow, and further appreciation. The goal is to use inflation to your advantage by acquiring properties that generate more income and appreciate faster, while deferring taxes that would otherwise be due if you simply sold your asset without reinvestment. This allows you to grow your portfolio more rapidly and keep more capital working for you.
- **Delay Depreciation Recapture** - Depreciation is a valuable tax deduction for real estate investors, but when you sell a property, you are typically required to "recapture" the depreciation and pay taxes on it. This can represent a significant tax liability, particularly if you've owned the property for a long time. A 1031 exchange provides a way to defer this depreciation recapture by rolling over your investment into a new property. As long as you continue to exchange and reinvest, you can defer this tax liability indefinitely, allowing you to maximize your returns in an inflationary market.

In summary, leveraging 1031 exchanges during periods of inflation enables you to defer taxes on rapidly appreciating assets, reinvest gains into more valuable properties, and avoid the immediate burden of depreciation recapture. By strategically upgrading and growing your portfolio in a rising market, you can maximize both your cash flow and asset value while keeping more of your money working for you.

Creative Financing Techniques and Inflation

In an inflationary environment, real estate investors may find traditional bank lending restrictive due to tightened lending criteria, increased interest rates, or their own limited credit capacity from rapid acquisitions.

Even when financing is available, you may want to move quickly and maximize leverage with limited down payments and flexible credit requirements associated with creative financing to take full advantage of rising property values and rents.

Creative financing options can provide flexible alternatives to traditional loans, enabling investors to grow their portfolios while managing cash flow and risk.

Here's a closer look at some common creative financing strategies:

- **Owner Financing** - In this arrangement, the seller acts as the lender, allowing you to make payments directly to them instead of a bank. This can offer more favorable terms, such as lower down payments, flexible interest rates, flexible credit requirements, or a customized payment schedule, making it easier to acquire properties without needing traditional financing.

- **Wrap Financing** - Also known as a wraparound mortgage, this structure allows you to take over the seller's existing mortgage while adding additional financing. The seller often continues making payments on the original loan, and you make payments to the seller that "wrap around" the existing mortgage. This can help secure properties with minimal upfront costs and allow you to benefit from potentially favorable existing loan terms.
- **Loan Assumption** - With a loan assumption, you take over the seller's existing mortgage with the lender's approval. This can be beneficial in a high-inflation environment if the original loan has a lower interest rate than current market rates. By assuming the loan, you may reduce your overall borrowing costs and preserve credit capacity. Usually a strategy for Nomads™ or house hackers since they often are for owner-occupants only.
- **The Rent-To-Own Family (Lease-Options, Lease-Purchases)** - These arrangements allow you to control a property with the option or obligation to purchase it at a later date. Lease-options and lease-purchases enable you to lock in today's property price while benefiting from any future appreciation. This approach often requires less upfront capital and offers flexibility, making it a valuable tool in high-inflation environments.
- **Agreement for Deed, Bond for Deed, Contract for Deed, Installment Land Contract Family** - These types of agreements allow you to make installment

payments directly to the seller while gaining equitable interest in the property over time. The seller retains legal title until the terms of the contract are fulfilled. This approach can offer more flexible financing terms, lower down payments, and bypass traditional lending hurdles.

- **Subject To** - In a subject-to deal, you take over the existing mortgage payments without formally assuming the loan. The seller's name remains on the mortgage, but you gain control of the property. This allows you to benefit from the original loan terms, such as a lower interest rate, which can be particularly advantageous when inflation drives up new loan rates. Subject-to deals often require less upfront cash and can preserve your credit capacity.

These creative financing techniques provide valuable options for real estate investors looking to move quickly, maximize leverage, and navigate the challenges of high inflation. By leveraging these strategies, you can acquire more properties with limited capital, maintain flexibility, and continue growing your portfolio despite market constraints.

Be careful with the added risk of taking on significant amounts of additional debt. Consider significantly increasing your reserves to help offset these additional risks.

BONUS CHAPTERS

Introduction to Real Estate Deal Analysis

Analyzing real estate deals can be a daunting task, but with the right tools and knowledge, it becomes much more manageable. One powerful tool we recommend is *The World's Greatest Real Estate Deal Analysis Spreadsheet*™. This spreadsheet is designed to help you evaluate the financial viability of real estate investments with ease and precision.

In our book, *How to Analyze Real Estate Deals*, we delve deep into the intricacies of deal analysis, providing step-by-step instructions and expert insights. This introduction aims to give you a high-level overview of the process and how to effectively use the spreadsheet to make informed investment decisions.

The spreadsheet allows you to input various data points such as purchase price, mortgage details, monthly income, and annual expenses. It then performs complex calculations to provide you with key metrics like cash flow, return on investment (ROI), and internal rate of return (IRR).

By leveraging this tool, you can:

- Quickly assess the profitability of potential deals.
- Compare multiple investment opportunities.
- Make data-driven decisions to maximize your returns.

Whether you're a seasoned investor or just starting out, understanding how to analyze real estate deals is crucial for success.

Download Spreadsheet for Free

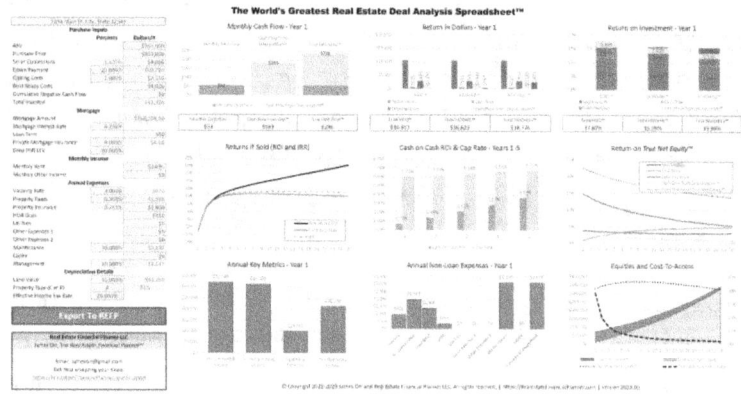

The World's Greatest Real Estate Deal Analysis Spreadsheet™

Unlock the full potential of your real estate investments by downloading *The World's Greatest Real Estate Deal Analysis Spreadsheet*™ for free.

Get your copy at: https://REFP.info/spreadsheet

We recommend always keeping an unedited, fresh copy on your hard drive in case you can't download the spreadsheet in the future.

Before analyzing a property, always make a new copy.

Spreadsheet Inputs

Entering the inputs into the spreadsheet is simple. Here's what you need to know:

- The manila fields indicate where you should input your data.
- The gray background with blue text shows the calculations that are automatically performed for you.

First, please name the deal that you're analyzing in the field just above the "Purchase Inputs". This will allow you to know which deal you're looking at if you're considering analyzing multiple deals or one deal multiple ways.

Purchase Inputs

Before we dive into the specifics of analyzing a real estate deal, let's go over the inputs required for the spreadsheet. These inputs will be divided into two columns: one for percentages and one for dollar amounts (or numbers).

Understanding what to enter in each field is crucial for accurately analyzing your deal. Let's go over what to put in each field next.

- **ARV** - Enter the After Repair Value, which is the estimated value of the property after all repairs and improvements have been made.
- **Purchase Price** - Enter the amount you are paying to acquire the property from the seller.
- **Seller Concessions** - Enter any financial concessions or incentives that the seller has agreed to provide, such as covering closing costs or offering repair credits.
- **Down Payment** - Enter the initial amount you will pay out-of-pocket towards the purchase of the property. Be sure to check out our guide on creative ways to come up with down payments for rental properties.
- **Closing Costs** - Enter the total costs associated with closing the real estate transaction, including title insurance, attorney fees, and other related expenses.
- **Rent Ready Costs** - Enter the expenses required to make the property ready for tenants, such as cleaning, repairs, and any necessary upgrades.
- **Cumulative Negative Cash Flow** - If you have negative cash flow enter the total cumulative amount of negative cash flow you anticipate before the property becomes cash flow positive. We recommend you set this aside to reduce risk. You may also want to check out our book on *How to Improve Cash Flow on Rental Properties* to get rid of negative cash flow on your properties.
- **Total Invested** - This is calculated for you. It is the cumulative amount of money you have invested in the

property, including **Down Payment, Closing Costs, Rent Ready Costs, Cumulative Negative Cash Flow,** minus any **Seller Concessions** you received from the seller.

Mortgage Inputs

To accurately analyze your real estate deal, it's essential to input detailed information about your mortgage and financing. These inputs will help calculate your monthly payments, interest costs, and overall financial commitment. Here's what you'll need to enter:

- **Mortgage Amount** - This is calculated for you. It is the total amount of money you are borrowing to finance the purchase of the property.
- **Mortgage Interest Rate** - Enter the annual interest rate for your mortgage. This is the percentage of the loan amount that you will pay as interest each year.
- **Loan Term** - Enter the duration of your mortgage loan in months. 360 months is a 30-year loan. This is the period over which you will repay the loan.
- **Private Mortgage Insurance** - Enter the monthly cost of private mortgage insurance (PMI) if applicable. PMI is typically required if your down payment is less than 20% of the purchase price. If you don't have PMI, use 0.000% here.
- **Drop PMI LTV** - Enter the loan-to-value (LTV) ratio at which PMI will be dropped. This is the point at which your equity in the property is high enough that PMI is no

longer required. If you don't have PMI, use 0.000% here.

Monthly Income

Accurately estimating your monthly income is critical for assessing the profitability of your real estate investment. This section will guide you through the necessary inputs for calculating your expected monthly income from the property, including rent and any additional sources of income.

- **Monthly Rent** - Enter the amount of rent you expect to receive from tenants each month. If you don't know how to determine what rent is on a property you're considering, you might want to check out our book on *How to Determine Rent Comps*.
- **Monthly Other Income** - Enter any additional monthly income from the property, such as parking fees, laundry services, or storage rentals.

Annual Expenses

Understanding and accurately estimating annual expenses is crucial for analyzing the financial viability of a real estate investment. This section will guide you through the various costs associated with owning and maintaining a property, from vacancy rates to property taxes and insurance. By thoroughly accounting for each of these expenses, you can better predict your investment's profitability and make more informed decisions.

- **Vacancy Rate** - Enter the percentage of time the property is expected to be vacant each year.
- **Property Taxes** - Enter the annual property tax amount you will pay for owning the property.
- **Property Insurance** - Enter the annual cost of insuring the property.
- **HOA Dues** - Enter the annual homeowner association fees, if applicable.
- **Utilities** - Enter the annual cost of utilities that you will pay as the property owner.
- **Other Expenses 1 and 2** - Enter any other annual expenses not covered in the previous categories.
- **Maintenance** - Enter the annual cost of maintaining the property, including repairs and routine upkeep.
- **CapEx** - Enter the annual amount set aside for capital expenditures. Consider our book and spreadsheet on CapEx for more guidance.
- **Management** - Enter the annual cost of property management services, if applicable.

Depreciation Details

Depreciation is a critical aspect of real estate investment analysis, as it allows you to account for the gradual reduction in the value of your property over time. Properly calculating and understanding depreciation can provide significant tax benefits and improve the overall financial picture of your investment. This section will guide you through the necessary inputs for determining depreciation, including land value, property type, and your effective income tax rate. By accurately inputting these details, you can optimize your investment strategy and maximize potential returns.

- **Land Value** - Enter the percent of the property that represents the value of the land. This value is used to calculate depreciation.
- **Property Type (C or R)** - Indicate whether the property is classified as commercial (C) or residential (R). This affects the depreciation schedule.
- **Effective Income Tax Rate** - Enter your effective income tax rate. This rate is used to estimate the tax benefits of depreciation.

Overrides

The spreadsheet is designed to be user-friendly on the Dashboard, while offering extensive functionality in the Overrides section. This dual approach ensures that users can easily navigate and input basic data, but also have access to more advanced features when needed.

In the Overrides tab, you have the ability to:

- **Modify any other inputs** - Adjust various parameters to suit your specific needs and scenarios.
- **Perform custom calculations** - Create and implement your own unique calculations to gain deeper insights into your investments.

- **View intermediate calculations** - Access detailed breakdowns of the calculations that drive the final results, providing transparency and better understanding.
- **Analyze performance over an extended period** - The spreadsheet allows you to conduct analysis through up to 40 years, enabling long-term strategic planning.
- **Track investment performance** - Use the Overrides tab to monitor how your investment evolves over time, making it easier to adjust your strategy as needed.

This comprehensive functionality ensures that the spreadsheet is not only a powerful tool for initial analysis but also a valuable resource for ongoing management and optimization of your real estate investments.

Dashboard

The Dashboard section provides a comprehensive overview of your real estate investment's key metrics and financial performance.

Here, you can quickly assess your monthly cash flow, return on investment (ROI), internal rate of return (IRR), and other critical indicators.

The Dashboard is designed to offer a user-friendly summary of your investment, allowing you to make informed decisions and track your progress over time.

Of course, you can dig into the Overrides tab for a ridiculous amount of additional detail.

Monthly Cash Flow - Year 1

This chart displays the Monthly Cash Flow, *Cash Flow from Depreciation*™, and the combined total, referred to as *True Cash Flow*™.

Understanding these metrics is crucial as they provide a comprehensive view of your investment's financial health.

- Monthly Cash Flow shows the actual cash inflow and outflow.
- *Cash Flow from Depreciation*™ accounts for tax benefits derived from property depreciation.
- *True Cash Flow*™ combines these figures, offering a more accurate representation of your investment's profitability.

Return in Dollars - Year 1

This chart displays the estimated dollars earned from your real estate investment over the first year, including Appreciation, Cash Flow, *Cash Flow from Depreciation*™, and Debt Paydown.

Understanding these metrics provides a holistic view of your investment's performance:

- **Appreciation** - Reflects the increase in property value over the year.
- **Cash Flow** - Shows the actual cash inflow and outflow.
- ***Cash Flow from Depreciation*™** - Accounts for tax benefits derived from property depreciation.

- **Debt Paydown** - Indicates the amount of principal paid down on your mortgage over the year.

Additionally, the chart includes earnings on reserves:

- **6 Months of Reserves in Savings** - Illustrates the interest earned if you set aside 6 months of reserves in a savings account.
- **Most of 12 Months of Reserves in Another Investment** - Shows the potential earnings if most of 12 months of reserves are invested in another investment vehicle like the stock market.

These combined figures provide a comprehensive representation of your investment's profitability and financial health over the first year.

You can see the totals at the bottom of the chart.

Return on Investment - Year 1

This chart displays the return on investment (ROI) from your real estate investment over the first year, including Appreciation, Cash Flow, *Cash Flow from Depreciation*™, and Debt Paydown.

Understanding these metrics provides a holistic view of your investment's performance:

- **Appreciation** - Reflects the increase in property value over the year divided by the total amount invested (and reserves where applicable).

- **Cash Flow** - Shows the actual cash inflow and outflow divided by the total amount invested (and reserves where applicable).
- ***Cash Flow from Depreciation***™ - Accounts for tax benefits derived from property depreciation divided by the total amount invested (and reserves where applicable).
- **Debt Paydown** - Indicates the amount of principal paid down on your mortgage over the year divided by the total amount invested (and reserves where applicable).

Additionally, the chart includes ROI on reserves:

- **6 Months of Reserves in Savings** - Illustrates the interest earned if you set aside 6 months of reserves in a savings account, divided by the total amount invested plus 6 months of reserves.
- **Most of 12 Months of Reserves in Another Investment** - Shows the potential earnings if most of 12 months of reserves are invested in another investment vehicle like the stock market, divided by the total amount invested plus 12 months of reserves.

These combined figures provide a comprehensive representation of your investment's profitability and financial health over the first year in terms of ROI.

You can see the totals at the bottom of the chart.

Returns if Sold (ROI and IRR)

This chart illustrates the return on investment if you sold the property each year for the first 20 years. It includes three key metrics:

- **Simple Annualized Return on Investment** - This metric shows the average annual return on your investment, calculated by dividing the total return by the number of years you held the property.
- **Compound Annualized Return on Investment** - This metric accounts for the compounding effect, showing the average annual return on your investment when considering the reinvestment of earnings.
- **Internal Rate of Return (IRR)** - This metric represents the annualized rate of return that makes the net present value (NPV) of all cash flows (both inflows and outflows) from the investment equal to zero.

These metrics provide a comprehensive view of the financial performance of your investment over time, helping you to understand the potential long-term profitability and compare it with other investment opportunities.

Cash on Cash ROI & Cap Rate - Years 1-5

This chart displays the Cash on Cash Return on Investment (ROI) and the Capitalization Rate (Cap Rate) for the property over the first 5 years.

Understanding these metrics provides a comprehensive view of your investment's performance:

- **Cash on Cash ROI** - This metric shows the annual return on your investment based on the actual cash invested. It is calculated by dividing the annual pre-tax cash flow by the total cash invested.
- **Cap Rate** - This metric represents the annual return on the property based on its current market value. It is calculated by dividing the net operating income (NOI) by the property's current market value.

By understanding these metrics, you can gauge the effectiveness and profitability of your investment, enabling you to make well-informed decisions and evaluate it against other potential investment opportunities.

Return on True Net Equity™

This chart shows you the returns you're earning from Appreciation, Cash Flow, *Cash Flow from Depreciation*™, and Debt Paydown divided by the equity minus the costs to access that equity with a sale (what we call True Net Equity™). It shows the first 20 years. It also shows the total of all four areas of return.

Understanding these metrics is crucial for assessing the true profitability of your real estate investment:

- **Appreciation** - Reflects the increase in property value over the year.
- **Cash Flow** - Shows the actual cash inflow and outflow.

- *Cash Flow from Depreciation*™ - Accounts for tax benefits derived from property depreciation.
- **Debt Paydown** - Indicates the amount of principal paid down on your mortgage over the year.

By dividing these returns by the True Net Equity™, you get a more accurate representation of your investment's performance, considering the costs to access the equity. This comprehensive view helps in making informed decisions and comparing the potential returns of different investments.

For more information on True Net Equity™ consider checking out our books about that:

- Should I Sell My Rental My Rental Property?
- Should I Sell My Refinance My Rental Property?

Annual Key Metrics - Year 1

This chart displays the financial performance of your real estate investment in terms of Gross Potential Income (GPI), Gross Operating Income (GOI), Operating Expenses (OpEx), and Net Operating Income (NOI) for the first year.

Understanding these metrics provides a comprehensive view of your investment's revenue and profitability:

- **Gross Potential Income (GPI)** - This metric represents the total income the property could generate if it were fully rented and all units were occupied at market rent rates, without accounting for any vacancies or losses.

- **Gross Operating Income (GOI)** - This metric reflects the actual income received from the property, including rent and other income sources, after accounting for vacancies and any collection losses.
- **Operating Expenses (OpEx)** - These are the costs associated with maintaining and managing the property, excluding mortgage payments and capital expenditures.
- **Net Operating Income (NOI)** - This metric is calculated by subtracting the operating expenses from the Gross Operating Income. It represents the income generated by the property after all operating expenses have been deducted.

By understanding these metrics, you can better assess the financial health and profitability of your real estate investment, helping you make more strategic decisions and compare it with other investment opportunities.

Annual Non-Loan Expenses - Year 1

This chart displays the financial performance of your real estate investment by itemizing all the non-loan expenses for the first year. Understanding these metrics provides a comprehensive view of your property's operational costs, which are crucial for accurate financial analysis and planning:

- **Vacancy Rate** - The percentage of time the property is expected to be vacant each year.
- **Property Taxes** - The annual amount paid for property taxes.

- **Property Insurance** - The cost of insuring the property for the year.
- **HOA Dues** - Annual homeowner association fees, if applicable.
- **Utilities** - The total annual cost of utilities paid by the property owner.
- **Other Expenses 1 and 2** - Any additional annual expenses not covered in the previous categories.
- **Maintenance** - The annual expense for maintaining the property, including routine repairs and upkeep.
- **CapEx** - The annual amount set aside for capital expenditures, such as major repairs or replacements.
- **Management Fees** - The cost of property management services, if utilized.

By breaking down these non-loan expenses, this chart helps you understand the total operational costs associated with your property, enabling you to better manage your investment and forecast its financial performance.

Equities and Cost-To-Access

This chart displays the equity in your real estate deal each year for the first 20 years, focusing on two key metrics: *True Net Equity*™ and Cash-Out Refi Equity.

- ***True Net Equity*™** - This is the equity minus the costs to access it through a sale. It shows the real profit after considering selling costs.

- **Cash-Out Refi Equity** - This is the equity available if you refinance the property. It helps you understand the potential funds available through refinancing.
- **Cost-To-Access Equity Percentages** - The chart also shows the costs (as a percentage of the equity) associated with accessing each type of equity. This provides insight into the expenses involved.

Understanding these metrics is crucial for knowing how much money you could pull out of the investment over time and the cost to access that equity if you choose to do so.

Trademarks: The World's Greatest Real Estate Deal Analysis Spreadsheet™, Cash Flow from Depreciation™, True Cash Flow, True Net Equity™, and Nomad™ are trademarks of James Orr and/or Real Estate Financial Planner LLC. All rights reserved.

94 Ways to Improve Cash Flow on Rental Properties

You might find yourself in a real estate market where:

- Property prices are high—possibly even soaring,
- Mortgage interest rates are elevated—maybe significantly so,
- Yet rents, despite any increases, haven't risen enough to offset these higher prices and rates.

Instead of the steady stream of cash flow you anticipated, you may be seeing just a trickle.

As a real estate broker, I developed the *Lowest Monthly Payment Guarantee*™ for my clients. This comprehensive checklist—backed by a *cash-in-your-pocket guarantee*—promised to uncover every possible way to reduce and minimize their monthly payments when purchasing a property.

For my real estate investor clients, I went a step further and created the *Maximum Cash Flow Guarantee*™. This second checklist—also backed by a *cash-in-your-pocket guarantee*—was designed to help them identify every possible way to increase and maximize the income generated from their rental properties.

Simply put, cash flow is the difference between income and expenses.

By maximizing income and minimizing expenses on a rental property, you can significantly boost your cash flow.

Below, you'll find an abridged version of these two checklists—combined into one—designed to help you maximize cash flow on your rental properties.

For your convenience, I've organized the strategies into seven distinct stages of the real estate investing process.

7 Distinct Real Estate Investing Stages for Improving Cash Flow

The real estate investing process can be broken down into seven distinct stages, each offering unique opportunities to improve cash flow:

1. **Searching for Properties** - Strategies to enhance cash flow while you're searching for a property to buy.

2. **Financing the Property** - Tactics to maximize cash flow when securing financing for the property you're purchasing.
3. **Improving the Real Estate Investing Strategy** - Different real estate investing strategies produce varying levels of cash flow. Here, you'll find strategies tailored to the specific investing approach you choose once you've acquired the property.
4. **Improving the Property** - Cash flow enhancement strategies based on making physical improvements to the property itself.
5. **Marketing the Property for Rent** - Techniques to boost cash flow during the process of marketing your property to prospective tenants.
6. **While Owning the Property** - Strategies you can implement at any time during ownership to optimize cash flow.
7. **While Renting the Property** - Methods to improve cash flow while actively renting out the property.

While applying strategies from each stage will maximize your cash flow, you can also focus on the stage you're currently in. Implement what you can now, and revisit these strategies regularly to continuously improve—aim for just a 1% improvement each month.

Searching for Properties

Here are the cash flow improving strategies to implement while searching for a property to buy.

- **Agent Selection** - Choosing the right real estate agent can have a significant impact on your investment's cash flow. Some agents offer lower commissions or commission rebates. This money can appear as improved cash flow in the first year or use the money to buy down your mortgage interest rate and get improved cash flow for the life of the loan.
- **Lock/Float** - When securing financing for a property, interest rates can fluctuate. Locking in an interest rate early can protect you from rising rates during the closing process, while floating allows you to benefit from potential rate drops. This decision can directly influence your cash flow by affecting your monthly mortgage payments. This is especially important when buying properties that have extended under contract periods like when buying new construction.
- **Search for Less Expensive Properties** - Lower-priced properties often come with smaller mortgage payments, which can improve cash flow if you're able to get the same rent as their more expensive alternatives. For every $10,000 less expensive the property, you save approximately $50 per month (when mortgage rates are in the 5% range). Some lower priced prices will have commensurately lower rents. Analyze each deal carefully to ensure that the overall income and expenses align to boost your cash flow.
- **Search for Pretty Properties** - Consider purchasing properties that are already in good condition and don't require significant fix-up costs. By doing so, you can allocate funds that would have been used for repairs to

increase your down payment or buy down the interest rate, both of which can lead to better cash flow.

- **Search for Seller Concessions** - Seller concessions are contributions from the seller to help cover your closing costs. By negotiating for these concessions, you can reduce your out-of-pocket expenses or even use them to buy down your mortgage interest rate, both of which enhance cash flow. Consider searching for properties that are offering seller concessions.
- **Search for Creative Financing** - Creative financing can offer more favorable terms than traditional loans, directly impacting your cash flow. Here are several types of creative financing to consider:

  - o **Search for Owner Financing** - Owner financing involves the seller acting as the lender, which can lead to better terms than a traditional bank loan. This can reduce your monthly payments and improve cash flow. We define owner financing as when the seller does not have a mortgage; if they have a mortgage that's wrap financing or buying the property subject to their existing mortgage which we will cover next.
  - o **Search for Wrap Financing** - In wrap financing, you agree to pay the seller a monthly amount that "wraps" around their existing mortgage. The seller keeps their original mortgage in place and continues making payments to their lender. You, in turn, make payments to the seller that cover both the existing mortgage and any additional amount you've agreed upon. This can result in a lower overall interest rate compared to obtaining new financing, which can

improve your cash flow. Wrap financing also gives the seller the protection of foreclosure rights if you fail to make payments.

- ○ **Search for Subject To**- In a "subject to" arrangement, you take ownership of the property while the seller's original mortgage stays in place. Instead of wrapping a new loan around the old one, you take over making payments directly to the lender on the seller's existing loan. The loan remains in the seller's name, but you're responsible for the payments. You're not formally accountable to the lender—it's not on your credit report—but you are responsible to the seller as per your agreement. This can be advantageous if the seller's mortgage has a lower interest rate than what's currently available. Like wrap financing, this can significantly reduce your mortgage expenses and boost cash flow. However, "subject to" financing typically doesn't offer the seller the same foreclosure protections as wrap financing does.
- ○ **Search for Assumable Loans** - Some loans can be formally transferred from the seller to the buyer, keeping the original interest rate intact. If the seller's loan has a lower interest rate, assuming the loan can significantly boost your cash flow. Since most loan assumptions are for owner-occupant borrowers this strategy likely only applies to those utilizing an owner-occupant investing strategy like house hacking or Nomad™.
- ○ **Search for Rent-To-Own Properties** - Rent-to-own agreements allow you to lease a property with the

option to purchase it later. These arrangements can offer lower initial payments and more flexible terms, which may improve your cash flow compared to traditional financing.

- o **Search for Agreements for Deed** - Also called bond for deed, contract for deed, or installment land contracts, these arrangements let you pay the seller directly over time. You get the deed after fulfilling the contract. This can lead to lower payments and improved cash flow while you're repaying.
- o **Search for Seller Financing** - Seller financing typically involves the seller offering a loan to cover a portion of the purchase price, often as a second mortgage or "carryback" loan. In this scenario, you would secure the primary mortgage from a traditional lender, and the seller finances the remaining balance. For example, if you purchase a property for $200,000, you might get a $160,000 loan from a bank, with the seller providing a $40,000 loan. This setup can result in more favorable terms, such as lower interest rates or flexible payment schedules, improving your overall cash flow. Unlike owner financing, where the seller finances the entire purchase, seller financing usually complements other financing sources, reducing the need for a larger bank loan.

Once you've found a promising property using the strategies above, the next step is to optimize your financing to further enhance your cash flow. Let's explore the various ways you can improve your cash flow during the financing stage of your real estate investment.

Financing the Property

Here are the cash flow improving strategies to implement while financing the property you're buying.

Before Getting Loan

Here are a few strategies to improve cash flow to use before getting your loan.

- **Lender Selection** - Shop around for lenders to find one that offers better interest rates, lower fees, or more favorable terms. Different lenders have varying costs and requirements, so comparing multiple options on the same day can ensure you get the best deal, improving your overall cash flow.
- **Select by Closing Costs** - Some loans come with higher closing costs than others. By selecting a loan with lower closing costs, especially if you plan to finance these costs, you can reduce the amount you need to borrow, leading to better cash flow due to lower monthly payments.
- **Lock/Float** - Decide whether to lock in your interest rate early to protect against potential rate increases before closing, or to float and take advantage of possible rate decreases. Locking your rate provides security, while floating offers flexibility, both of which can impact your cash flow depending on market conditions.

- **Offer Less** - Negotiating a lower purchase price directly reduces the amount you need to finance, leading to lower monthly mortgage payments. This strategy can also leave more of your resources available for other cash flow improvement tactics.

Pay Upfront Instead of Financing

Here are some strategies for improving cash flow that deal with opting to pay fees upfront instead of financing them.

- **Seller Concessions** - Negotiate for the seller to cover some of your closing costs or to provide credits that can be used to buy down your mortgage interest rate. This is almost certainly required to be done at the time you make your offer and not after your offer is accepted. This reduces your upfront cash outlay and can lower your monthly mortgage payments, thereby improving cash flow.
- **Pay Closing Costs** - Paying your closing costs upfront instead of rolling them into your mortgage can reduce the amount you borrow, lowering your monthly payments and improving cash flow over the life of the loan.
- **Pre-Pay PMI** - If you're required to pay Private Mortgage Insurance (PMI), consider pre-paying it in a lump sum rather than monthly. This reduces your ongoing monthly expenses, leading to better cash flow.
- **Staggered Rate** - Opt for a staggered interest rate loan, where the interest rate is lower in the initial years

and increases over time. This can provide you with better cash flow during the early years of the loan when you may need it most.

- **Buy Down Rate** - Pay upfront to lower your mortgage interest rate for the life of the loan. A lower interest rate means a lower monthly payment, which can significantly improve your cash flow over time. For long-term buy and hold real estate investors—especially if you find yourself in a low mortgage interest rate environment—this can be an amazing strategy.

Change/Improve Borrower(s)

These strategies for improving cash flow relate to changing or improving the borrower on the loan.

- **Credit Score** - Improving your credit score can help you secure a lower interest rate and reduce your PMI rate. Both of these improvements lead to lower monthly payments and better cash flow.
- **Add Borrower** - Adding a co-borrower with a strong credit profile to your loan can help you qualify for a better interest rate and lower PMI, both of which can enhance your cash flow.
- **Remove Borrower** - If one borrower has a weaker credit profile, removing them from the loan might result in a better interest rate. This can lead to lower monthly payments and improved cash flow.
- **Loan Partner** - Partnering with someone who has a strong financial profile can help you secure better loan

terms, including lower interest rates and more favorable conditions, which ultimately enhance your cash flow.

Relationship With Lender

These cash flow improving strategies are based on your relationship with the lender or lending institution.

- **Auto Pay Loan** - Setting up automatic payments can sometimes qualify you for a slight reduction in your interest rate, directly improving your cash flow by lowering your monthly mortgage payment. It may show up also as a penalty to the interest rate if you don't use autopay for the mortgage.
- **Additional Accounts** - Maintaining additional accounts or depositing more funds with your lender might earn you a small interest rate reduction, leading to improved cash flow through lower monthly payments. This is more common with commercial loans and relationship banking.

Change Amortization

These strategies to improve your cash flow deal with changing the amortization schedule of the financing you're getting.

- **Interest Only** - An interest-only loan allows you to pay only the interest for a certain period, which significantly reduces your monthly payments. This can boost your cash flow in the short term, though it comes with long-term risks since the principal remains unpaid. You'll need to have a solid plan to deal with the loan balance when the ballon payment date arrives.

- **Negative Amortization** - A negative amortizing loan allows you to pay less than the interest due, causing the loan balance to increase over time. This lowers your initial payments and improves short-term cash flow but increases your debt over time.
- **Rate from Loan Term** - Shortening the loan term (e.g., switching from a 30-year to a 15-year mortgage) can lower your interest rate. However, this typically increases your monthly payments, so it's more about long-term savings than immediate cash flow improvement.
- **Loan Term** - Extending the loan term (e.g., from 30 to 40 years) reduces the monthly payment amount, which can improve your cash flow. However, this means you'll pay more interest over the life of the loan.

Loan Terms

These cash flow improving strategies deal with the terms (details) of the loan itself.

- **Amount Borrowed** - Putting more money down reduces the amount you need to borrow, leading to lower monthly payments. This can improve your cash flow, though it also means tying up more capital in the property.

- **Loan-To-Value** - A lower loan-to-value (LTV) ratio, achieved by making a larger down payment, often results in a better interest rate. This lowers your monthly payments and improves cash flow. Not only can putting more down improve your LTV and give you a better interest rate, but it might also reduce your Private Mortgage Insurance (PMI) payment since that's part of the calculation for determining PMI amounts.
- **Adjustable Rate** - An adjustable-rate mortgage (ARM) typically starts with a lower interest rate than a fixed-rate mortgage. This can enhance your cash flow in the initial years, though the rate—and your payments—can increase later.

Private Mortgage Insurance (PMI)

These strategies to improve cash flow deal primarily with Private Mortgage Insurance (PMI).

What is PMI? The lender would prefer you put at least 20% down to finance a property. With 20% down they feel comfortable enough that if you don't pay as agreed they will be able to foreclose, sell the property and get all their money back after the expenses of foreclosure and sale.

You insist on putting less than 20% down.

They may reluctantly agree, but they may charge you a higher interest rate because it is a riskier loan to them. And, additionally, they may insist that you pay a third-party insurance company a fee that insures them in case you default and they're unable to foreclose and sell the property to recoup their entire investment. This third-party insurance company is Private Mortgage Insurance.

It is insurance you pay for to protect the lender in case you default on the loan.

- **Eliminate PMI** - If you can put down at least 20% of the purchase price, you can avoid PMI altogether, significantly reducing your monthly mortgage expenses and improving your cash flow.
- **Pre-Pay PMI** - Paying PMI in a lump sum upfront instead of monthly can reduce your ongoing costs, leading to better cash flow throughout the loan term.
- **Improve Credit** - Enhancing your credit score can help you secure a lower PMI rate or even eliminate PMI altogether if your LTV ratio improves, both of which contribute to better cash flow.
- **Add Borrowers** - Added a borrower to your loan typically reduces PMI and therefore improves cash flow.

Other Properties

These cash flow improving strategies rely on tapping into other properties you own.

Some of these strategies deal with making sure your cash flow is optimized for your entire portfolio (including these other properties) and not specifically to a new property you're buying.

- **Cash Out Refi to Buy/Refi** - Consider doing a cash-out refinance on another property to use the proceeds for purchasing or refinancing your current property. This can result in better overall financing terms and improved cash flow.
- **Cash Out Refi for Larger Down Payment** - If putting more down on your current property will secure a better interest rate or eliminate PMI, consider using funds from a cash-out refinance on another property. This can lower your monthly payments and improve cash flow.
- **Rate and Term Before Acquisition** - Before purchasing a new property, consider refinancing your existing properties to better terms. As you own more properties the complexity of refinancing increases significantly. Consider this a reminder to consider this before each new purchase and to make any changes to other properties now before you add a new property that further limits what you can do. This can also improve the overall cash flow on your portfolio and might also allow you to qualify for better financing on the new purchase.

Non-Traditional Financing

These are some non-traditional financing strategies for improving cash flow you might want to consider.

- **Pay Cash** - If you have sufficient funds, paying cash for a property eliminates the need for financing altogether, which maximizes cash flow by removing monthly mortgage payments.

- **Private Financing** - Secure a loan from family or friends (private lenders) who might offer more favorable terms than traditional banks. This can lead to lower monthly payments and improved cash flow.
- **Creative Financing** - Explore options like owner financing, wrap financing, agreement for deed, lease-options, or subject to, where the seller might offer better terms than traditional lenders. These strategies can lower your mortgage payments and enhance cash flow.
- **Assumable Loan** - If the seller's existing loan has a lower interest rate than current market rates, assuming their loan can be a great way to secure better financing terms, leading to improved cash flow. This is more likely for owner-occupant loans, so this is probably limited to owner-occupant investing strategies like house hacking or Nomad™.

While optimizing your financing is crucial for improving cash flow, it's equally important to consider how your chosen real estate investing strategy can impact your returns. Let's now explore various strategies that can enhance your cash flow by refining your overall investment approach.

Improving the Real Estate Investing Strategy

Here are the cash flow improving strategies based on improving the real estate investing strategy you're opting to utilize.

- **Term** - Adjusting the duration of your lease can significantly impact your cash flow. Shorter-term rentals, such as daily, weekly, or monthly leases, often command higher rents compared to yearly leases. However, shorter terms can also lead to increased expenses, including higher vacancy rates, more frequent marketing, and potentially higher management and maintenance costs. Offering different terms, such as furnished vs. unfurnished rentals, can also cater to various market segments, like vacation rentals or boarding houses, providing opportunities to maximize income.

- **Lease-Option** - Lease-option strategies, including variations like rent-to-own (like lease-purchases and lease-options), can dramatically improve cash flow, particularly in markets where buying is significantly more expensive than renting. These arrangements typically involve collecting a non-refundable purchase deposit/option fee, which can—mathematically—appear to add hundreds of dollars per month to your cash flow. Additionally, tenants in lease-option agreements often treat the property with more care, reducing maintenance, vacancy, and management costs. This strategy is a form of our *Deal Alchemy*™, where you trade future appreciation returns for immediate cash flow.

- **Niche** - Specializing in a specific rental market can allow you to charge premium rents by catering to unique needs. For example, you might focus on corporate rentals, traveling nurses, or student housing. By understanding and addressing the specific requirements of your niche audience, such as providing furnished units for corporate rentals or flexible leases for students, you can add value that justifies higher rental rates. The key is to determine what additional services or amenities you can offer that will attract your target market and what premium you can reasonably charge for those services.

The following cash flow improving strategies are really just variations of house hacking where you're renting out part of the property you're living in for income and to improve cash flow. However, you could utilize these strategies even when you're not living in the property.

- **Roommates** - Renting out individual bedrooms in a single-family home, or additional units in a duplex, triplex, or fourplex, can significantly increase your cash flow. This is a common house hacking strategy where you live in one part of the property and rent out the rest. For example, you might rent out spare bedrooms in your own home or lease the other units in a multi-family property. This approach allows you to maximize the rental income from a single property by utilizing every available space.

- **Rent by Bed/Bedroom** - Some properties, particularly those near colleges or universities, may lend themselves well to renting by the bedroom or even by the bed. This strategy works particularly well with student housing, where multiple tenants share a single property. By renting out each bedroom or bed individually, you can often achieve a higher overall rent compared to leasing the entire property to a single tenant.

- **Rent by Parts** - Renting out different parts of a property, such as non-conforming units in a duplex, triplex, or fourplex, can be a lucrative strategy. It's essential to check local occupancy laws to ensure compliance. This strategy can also include more unconventional setups, such as renting out RV parking spaces, tiny homes, garages, or storage units on the property. These spaces don't have to be residential; they can be rented for commercial or recreational purposes, such as storage or use of shared community amenities like a pool or recreational center.

While optimizing your real estate investing strategy can significantly boost cash flow, another powerful approach is to enhance the property itself. By making strategic improvements and modifications to your rental property, you can potentially increase its value and appeal, leading to higher rental income and improved cash flow. Let's explore some effective strategies for improving cash flow through property enhancements.

Improving the Property

Here are the cash flow improving strategies based on making improvements to the property.

- **Subdivide** - Consider subdividing your property into multiple units to increase rental income. For example, you could rent the upstairs and downstairs separately, offering tenants more privacy while still sharing common areas like heating, cooling, mail, laundry, and possibly even the kitchen or living areas. This isn't the same as converting the property into a formal duplex or triplex; instead, it's more about creating a roommate-like situation with more separation. This setup allows you to comply with local roommate laws and zoning requirements while potentially charging higher rents, as tenants may feel like they have their own space.
- **Upgrade Property** - Enhancing your property's curb appeal and overall condition can justify charging higher rents. Improvements could include landscaping, painting, adding or improving shutters, lawn care, updating the mailbox, property address numbers, or exterior lighting. These upgrades can attract higher-paying tenants and increase the property's value. This approach is also common in value-add strategies or the BRRRR (Buy, Rehab, Rent, Refinance, Repeat) method, where the goal is to improve the property to increase its rent and overall profitability.
- **Solar** - Installing solar panels and including the cost of electricity in the base rent can make your property more attractive to tenants who value energy efficiency,

potentially allowing you to charge higher rents. However, you should be cautious about the legal implications of charging for utilities, as this can sometimes enter a gray area. It's advisable to consult with a local attorney to ensure compliance with utility billing regulations.

- **Furnished Rental** - Offering a furnished rental can significantly increase the rent you can charge, especially if you shift your strategy to short-term or medium-term rentals, such as vacation rentals, student rentals, or corporate housing. Furnished rentals appeal to tenants looking for convenience and are often willing to pay a premium for a move-in ready home.

- **Convert Property** - Converting a single-family property into a duplex, triplex, or fourplex can increase your rental income by creating multiple rental units within the same property. This approach is especially effective if the property is already somewhat set up for such a conversion. However, it may be cost-prohibitive or even impossible if significant structural changes are required or if zoning laws restrict such conversions. Always check with your city and county regarding zoning and licensing requirements before starting any conversion work, as this can also affect the types of loans you can secure and their terms, including the loan-to-value ratio.

- **Improvement Rent** - Charging extra rent for specific property improvements can help offset the cost of upgrades while increasing your overall rental income. For example, you might charge a tenant more for installing new carpet or a fence. While you may not be able to recoup the full cost of the improvement from a single tenant, some upgrades, like a fence, can justify higher rents with future tenants as well, allowing you to gradually recover your investment and potentially earn a return. This strategy is particularly useful for items with a long lifespan, where the cost can be spread out over multiple tenancies.

While property improvements can significantly boost your rental income, the way you market your property can be equally important for maximizing cash flow. By implementing effective marketing strategies, you can attract high-quality tenants, reduce vacancy periods, and potentially command higher rents. Let's explore some key strategies for improving cash flow through smart marketing techniques.

Marketing the Property for Rent

Here are the cash flow improving strategies to implement while you're marketing your property for rent.

- **Optimize Marketing** - Effective marketing starts with high-quality materials. Ensure that you have professional-grade photos, a 3D tour, and a video to showcase your property. These elements can significantly enhance the appeal of your listing, attracting more potential tenants. Additionally, use online marketing as well as flyers and signs strategically around the neighborhood to increase visibility. Well-designed marketing materials make your property stand out and convey a sense of professionalism that can justify higher rent and reduce vacancy periods.

- **Maximize Exposure** - To attract the right tenants, it's crucial to advertise your property across all available platforms where tenants might be searching. This includes online rental websites, social media, and community bulletin boards. Physical advertising, such as yard signs and directional signs leading to the property, can also capture the attention of local renters. By maximizing exposure, you increase the chances of filling vacancies quickly and with quality tenants.

- **Sales Skills** - Mastering sales skills is essential for renting your property at the highest possible rate and minimizing vacancy. This includes both phone skills for initial inquiries and in-person salesmanship during property tours. Being persuasive and knowledgeable helps you connect with potential tenants, address their concerns, and highlight the property's best features, ultimately leading to faster lease agreements and better tenant retention.

- **Optimize Showings** - Preparing your property for showings is a key step in securing a lease. Ensure the property is well-lit, smells pleasant, and is clean, neat, and in good repair. First impressions matter, and a well-presented property can make the difference between a potential tenant choosing your property over another. Additionally, create a sense of scarcity by scheduling back-to-back showings and mentioning this when booking appointments. This strategy can create urgency and increase interest among prospective tenants.

While effective marketing strategies can help attract tenants and maximize rental income, it's equally important to focus on optimizing your property's financial performance during ownership. Let's explore various strategies you can implement to improve cash flow throughout your tenure as a property owner.

While Owning the Property

Here are the cash flow improving strategies to implement while you own the property.

Refi/Pay Off Loan

Managing your mortgage can be one of the most effective ways to improve cash flow and overall property profitability.

- **Refi to Extend Term** - If your loan is old enough, consider refinancing to extend the loan term. This can lower your monthly payments and—if interest rates have dropped and/or your loan-to-value has improved—potentially secure a better interest rate, improving your cash flow.
- **Refi to Improve Rate** - If interest rates have dropped since you first took out your mortgage, refinancing to a lower rate can reduce your monthly payments and save you money over the life of the loan.
- **Payoff Loan** - If you have the financial means, paying off your loan in its entirety can eliminate your mortgage payments, drastically improving your monthly cash flow and reducing financial stress.

Taxes

Property taxes are a significant expense for any property owner, and managing them effectively can save you money.

- **Correct Assessor** - Ensure that the county assessor has accurate information about your property's condition and characteristics. Correcting any inaccuracies can prevent overvaluation and keep your taxes in check.
- **Contest Tax Increases** - If your property taxes increase, consider contesting the increase. Successful challenges can lead to reduced tax bills and improved cash flow.
- **Vote** - Participate in local elections and vote on measures that affect property taxes. Being informed and voting appropriately can help control future tax increases.

Insurance

Insurance is essential for protecting your investment, but it's also an area where you can manage costs.

- **Shop Insurance Rates** - Regularly compare insurance rates from different providers to ensure you're getting the best deal. Competitive rates can lower your insurance costs without sacrificing coverage.
- **Insurance Coverage** - Review your property insurance policy to make sure you have the right level of coverage. Avoid overpaying for unnecessary coverage or underinsuring your property. It is not just about

minimizing this cost while sacrificing coverage; you must make sure you minimize cost while keeping a desirable level of coverage. Sacrificing coverage is short-sighted and might significantly hurt cash flow if you ever have a claim that is you opted not to cover.

- **Insured** - Adjust your insurance policy by adding or removing people as needed to optimize your rates. This can lead to lower premiums.
- **Insurance Deductible** - Consider raising your deductible to lower your insurance premium. Taking on more risk personally can reduce your monthly insurance costs. See comments about sacrificing coverage being short-sighted above.
- **Remove PMI** - Totally different type of insurance, but if your property's equity has increased sufficiently, you may be able to remove Private Mortgage Insurance (PMI). This can significantly reduce your monthly mortgage payment.

Making Payments

How you manage your payments can also impact your overall costs.

- **Discount for Autopay** - Sign up for autopay on utilities and other bills to avoid per-bill fees. Many service providers offer small discounts or waive fees for customers who enroll in autopay.
- **Discount for Early Payments** - Some service providers, such as HOA or insurance companies, offer

discounts for early payments. Paying these bills in advance can reduce your overall expenses.

Management

Whether you manage your property yourself or hire a professional, effective management is key to maintaining profitability.

- **Self-Manage** - If you choose to manage the property yourself, ensure you stay up to date with the latest laws, best practices, and compliance issues. Self-management can save on property management fees, but it often requires a significant time investment.
- **Professional Property Manager** - Shop around for a high-quality property manager who offers reasonable fees. A good property manager can maximize your rental income and minimize headaches.
- **Manage the Manager** - Even with a professional property manager, it's important to regularly review management statements for accuracy. Mistakes can happen, and catching them early can save you money.
- **Insist on Best Practices** - Ensure your property manager follows best practices, such as marketing your property early and raising rents with each lease renewal. This proactive approach can help maximize your rental income.

Maintenance

Regular maintenance is crucial for keeping your property in good condition and minimizing vacancies.

- **Maintain Property** - Regularly maintaining your property can reduce the time it spends vacant between tenants. A well-maintained property attracts tenants quickly and reduces downtime.
- **Quality Materials** - Using quality materials for maintenance and repairs may have a higher upfront cost, but it can lower the overall cost of maintenance over time by reducing the frequency of repairs and replacements.

Depreciation

Depreciation can provide significant tax benefits, and managing it strategically can enhance your investment returns.

- **Accelerate Depreciation** - Consider accelerating depreciation on your property to maximize tax benefits in the short term. This strategy can improve your cash flow by reducing your taxable income, but it should be used with careful planning to avoid potential future tax liabilities. This can be one of the larger improvements to your cash flow.

While the strategies for improving cash flow during property ownership are crucial, it's equally important to optimize your rental income while renting it. Let's explore various techniques you can implement to enhance your cash flow during the rental phase of your investment.

While Renting the Property

Here are the cash flow improving strategies to implement while you're renting the property.

Add Services

Offering additional services can increase rental income and enhance tenant satisfaction.

- **Additional Services** - Consider offering additional services such as high-speed internet, cable, or utilities for an extra fee. Tenants often value the convenience of bundled services, making this an effective way to boost your rental income. However, be sure to check local laws, as this practice may not be permitted in some areas.
- **DFY Services** - Offer done-for-you (DFY) services such as lawn care, snow removal, or house cleaning. These services can be billed as extras, appealing to tenants who prefer convenience and are willing to pay for it.

Charge Appropriately

Setting appropriate charges can maximize your rental income while offering flexibility to tenants.

- **Bill Back** - Implement bill-back strategies for utilities or HOA services, such as charging tenants for non-potable water or other shared resources. This helps to ensure that tenants are covering their fair share of costs, improving your net income.
- **Tier Rent by Credit Score** - Adjust rent based on the tenant's credit score, with higher rent for those with lower scores. This can also apply to security deposits, where tenants with better credit pay less upfront. Check with your attorney before implementing this strategy.
- **Pet Rent** - Charge additional rent for tenants with pets. Pet rent can help cover potential wear and tear caused by pets and increase your overall rental income.

Convenience Billing

Convenience billing options can make it easier for tenants to pay rent while potentially increasing your revenue.

- **Billing Frequency** - Offer more frequent billing options, such as weekly or biweekly payments, instead of the traditional monthly schedule. This can be attractive to tenants who prefer smaller, more manageable payments but can also produce more cash flow over the same period.
- **Autopay** - Here are conflicting ideas where both options may ultimately improve cash flow. Encourage tenants to enroll in autopay by offering a discount or, conversely, charge a fee for those who do not use autopay. Autopay

can reduce late payments and ensure consistent cash flow.

- **Discount On-Time Payment** - Provide a discount for tenants who pay their rent on time or early, incentivizing prompt payments and reducing the need for late payment penalties.
- **Term** - Adjust the term of rental agreements to fit different rental strategies. Consider offering daily, weekly, or short-term/vacation rentals, which can often command higher rents than traditional monthly leases.

Timing

Optimizing the timing of lease agreements and renewals can minimize vacancies and maximize rental income.

- **Notice** - Require a 60-90 day notice from tenants if they intend not to renew their lease. This provides you with ample time to market the property and secure a new tenant, reducing vacancy periods.
- **Start Early/Test Rent** - Begin marketing the property early, even before the current tenant moves out, and start with a higher rent to test the market. This strategy allows you to adjust pricing based on demand and secure the best possible rental rate.
- **Renew Peak Season** - Align lease renewal dates to end during peak rental seasons, such as spring or summer, when demand is higher. This increases the likelihood of filling the property quickly and possibly at a higher rent.

Miscellaneous

Implementing additional requirements can protect your property and reduce potential liabilities.

- **Renter's Insurance** - Require tenants to carry renter's insurance. This protects both you and the tenant in case of damage to the property or loss of personal belongings, reducing potential conflicts and liabilities.

Conclusion

This guide has explored 94 ways to improve cash flow on rental properties across seven distinct stages of your real estate investing process.

Each stage presents unique opportunities to boost your investment's financial performance, and the cumulative effect of applying these strategies can significantly increase your property's profitability.

By focusing on cash flow improvement at every stage, you can:

- Build a more resilient and profitable real estate portfolio
- Enhance property values—especially for properties where value is driven by the income they generate, such as commercial properties
- Strengthen your ability to secure favorable financing by improving loan-to-value (LTV) and debt service coverage ratios
- Optimize tax benefits

- Accelerate savings for larger down payments and quickly replenish reserves
- Increase tenant satisfaction by enhancing the tenant experience, improving retention rates, and reducing turnover costs

Remember, even small adjustments across multiple areas can compound into substantial gains in your overall returns and financial stability.

Make it a habit to regularly review and implement these strategies, tailoring them to fit your specific properties and market conditions.

With consistent effort and strategic application, you can transform your rental properties into powerful, cash-generating assets that support your long-term financial goals.

Introduction to Monte Carlo Analysis of Rental Properties

There's a problem with how we've been modeling our investments so far. It is not unique to us. Almost everyone does it wrong.

But, we're going to fix it now.

The issue is the assumptions we've been using and how the real world works.

For the analysis we've been doing with *The World's Greatest Real Estate Deal Analysis Spreadsheet*™ (TWGREDAS)—and any other real estate deal analysis spreadsheet—we've used static assumptions.

We might assume that property values are going up by 3% per year. Well, that's not truly a correct representation of reality.

Heck, with the overrides tab in TWGREDAS we may have said, they go up by 3% for the first 3 years and then only 2% thereafter. Better, but still not reality.

The truth is: we really don't know how much property values will go up as we hold the property. They could go up by 3%. They could go down by 3%. They could go up then down or down then up. Could be more or less than 3%. Might be 3.1% or 2.9%. Might be up or down 6% or 10%.

If we look back at history (and we do when we consider the risks of investing in real estate), we can see what property appreciation has done over the last 100 years.

Risk Matrix: Appreciation

Severity					
	0	1	2	3	4
Likelihood	Increase	Small Decline	Medium Decline	Large Decline	Catastrophic
1	>10% Increase 7.7%			10-15% Decline 6.0%	>15% Decline 0.0%
2	5-10% Increase 15.0%		5-10% Decline 12.8%		
3	0-5% Increase 25.6%	0-5% Decline 34.6%			

So, to correctly model how our investment might perform, we should not use a static 3% per year—or whatever static number you believe to be true—for property appreciation.

Our crystal balls are broken. We can't accurately predict—exactly—what appreciation will be for our properties.

We can guess. Based on what has happened in the past they will average about 3% per year.

But they may:

- Increase in value by more than 10% for the year about 7.7% of the time
- Increase between 5% and 10% for the year about 15% of the time
- Increase between 0% and 5% for the year about 25.6% of the time
- Go down in value between 0% and 5% for the year about 34.6% of the time

- Go down in value between 5% and 10% for the year about 12.8% of the time
- Go down in value between 10% and 15% for the year about 6% of the time

These are based on what has happened over the last 100 years. Could the future be different? Absolutely.

But it is much more accurate than just assuming that they will be going up in value by 3% per year every year.

Not Just Property Appreciation

As you probably guessed, this isn't just an issue with property appreciation. It applies to other assumptions we have as well.

Here's a list of some of the more significant ones:

- **Property Appreciation Rate** - This is the one we've been talking about already. It is how much properties go up or down in value.
- **Rent Appreciation Rate** - This is how much rents increase or decrease with each lease renewal.
- **Inflation Rate** - Inflation reflects the overall increase in prices and the decrease in purchasing power over time. It impacts everything from the cost of goods and services to the value of money itself. In the context of your portfolio, inflation affects how much your money will be worth in the future, influencing the real returns on your investments. For instance, even if your rental

income and property values rise, high inflation could erode those gains in terms of actual purchasing power. A million dollars today isn't the same as a million dollars 50 years ago and it won't be the same as a million dollars 50 years from now.

- **Mortgage Interest Rates** - **Mortgage Interest Rates** - Mortgage rates fluctuate over time. The rate you secure for your current property purchase or refinance won't necessarily be the same for properties you buy in one, five, or more years from now.
- **Stock Market Rate of Return** - This is how much you're earning on money you have invested in the stock market. This also applies to other investments you might have like savings accounts, bonds, CDs, cryptocurrencies, etc.

If you really want to go to freaky town, you could also model this with changing tax rates, insurance rates, maintenance and capital expenses on the property.

Does This Even Matter?

Does this even matter and why should I care?

Let's start with a simple example of someone who invests in stocks. They don't even buy a home to live in; they rent instead.

They invest approximately 10% of their income in the stock market earning 8% per year.

Using static assumptions, we could calculate that they would be financially independent (FI) after about 53.25 years.

See **Error! Reference source not found.** at the end of the chapter. We moved the charts to the end of the chapter—instead of inline—so we could show you larger, readable versions of the charts.

But what if we used a reasonable range of values for the return from the stock market instead of always 8% every year?

We could use a range of values that better approximates what the stock markets has done historically—still averaging about 8% for this selection of stocks.

Instead of seeing a smooth line showing their journey toward financial independence as shown in Error! Reference source not found. at the end of the chapter.

We'd instead see a less smooth line representing how the stock market returns change each month like Error! Reference source not found..

And, if we ran it 10 times, you'd see that when they actually achieve financial independence (when the line crosses the horizontal dotted line) is a little different each time. See Error! Reference source not found..

If the stock market performs well, they're financially independent earlier. If the stock market does not perform as well, they end up being financially independent later.

If we ran this 1,000 times and summarized the results, we can see the range of when they're financially independent. See Error! Reference source not found..

Monte Carlo Modeling

This type of analysis is called Monte Carlo modeling.

Monte Carlo modeling is a statistical technique used to simulate multiple potential outcomes for an investment or financial scenario.

It works by:

- Running hundreds or thousands of simulations with varying input parameters
- Analyzing the range and probability of different outcomes
- Providing a more nuanced understanding of potential risks and returns

For real estate investing, Monte Carlo analysis involves varying input factors such as property appreciation rates, rent increases, mortgage interest rates, inflation, and market returns. This approach allows you to better assess the likelihood of achieving your financial goals and understand the potential risks associated with your investment strategies.

I like to call it *Alternate Universe Modeling*™ because we're consider how your investments might perform if you were living in alternate universes with different futures.

Back to our example with someone just investing in stocks.

In Error! Reference source not found. at the end of the chapter:

- The light blue band shows the full range of results from the very worst to the very best.
- The darker blue band in the middle shows you the middle 50% of all runs. Half of the time the results are this darker band.
- The dark link at the very center shows you the median value. Half the values are higher than this. Half the values are lower than this.

If we look at the median line we can see that half the time they're financially independent around 58 years. Half the time it is after 58 years.

It could have been as early as year 48. And, it could take longer than 60 years—when we stopped modeling for this example. In fact, only about 85% of the 1,000 runs we ran were financially independent 60 years from when they started.

We can summarize this is a different chart and show what percentage of the 1,000 runs were financially independent in each month. That's Error! Reference source not found..

By using a range of values for things like the stock market rate of return, we get a much more nuanced understanding of what is likely to happen.

What If They Became Homeowners Instead of Renting?

Our last example they were renting a property to live in and investing in stocks.

What if they bought on owner-occupant property with 5% down to live in and invested in stocks?

If we used static assumptions they would be financially independent about 15 and half years faster as shown in Error! Reference source not found. at the end of the chapter.

Part of what gets them to financial independence faster is that they end up paying off their owner-occupant property 30 years after they buy it. Without a mortgage payment the threshold for them being financially independent is a little lower.

There's a little more to this story, but I don't want to go off into the weeds here. The punchline is they achieve financial independence faster with static assumptions as you can see in Error! Reference source not found..

Let's vary the property appreciation rate, mortgage interest rate, inflation rate, and stock market rate of return. If we were discussing rentals, we'd vary the rent appreciation rate as well but in this case they're not buying any rentals; we'll get to that shortly.

With variable property appreciation rates, mortgage interest rates until they lock in a 30-year fixed rate financing loan, inflation rate and stock market rate of return it looks like Error! Reference source not found..

They're financially independent as early as 33.75 years from when they start. In 99.5% of the 1,000 runs they're financially independent by the time we stop modeling at 60 years.

How does this compare to them just investing in stocks? Let's show both on one chart in Error! Reference source not found..

Buying an owner-occupant property seems to make a pretty big difference.

If we just look at what percentage of the 1,000 runs they achieve financial independence, you can see that buying the owner-occupant property is more probable (higher percentage of the runs achieve it) and they're financially independent earlier (it happens more to the left on the chart). See Error! Reference source not found..

Buying Rental Properties with 20% Down Payments

Let's assume, for now, that they don't buy an owner-occupant property with 5% down. Instead, they decide to buy 20% down rental properties as their primary investing strategy.

Any additional money beyond what they need for the rentals is still investing in stocks, but whenever they get enough for a 20% down payment they buy a rental property with very modest cash flow.

They're willing to buy up to ten 20% down payment rentals.

If we have **static assumptions** for property appreciation, rent appreciation, inflation, mortgage interest rates and the stock market rate of return, they might be financially independent after 31 years.

With static assumptions, that's about 18.67 years faster than just investing in stocks and about 3 years faster than buying an owner-occupant property and investing stocks as shown in Error! Reference source not found..

With static assumptions, they achieve financial independence faster. See Error! Reference source not found..

And, still looking at the chart above, they appear have a lot more income coming then just investing in stocks the longer they hold the rental properties.

In fact, they're earning about twice what they need to be financially independent about 48.5 years in. That means they're earning twice what they need to be financially independent before just investing in stocks as a renter is even earning enough for them to financially independent at all.

Not long after they achieve financial independence just investing in stocks as a renter, they're earning 3 times what they need to be financially independent with their 10 rentals.

But, this is about Monte Carlo modeling, so what if we did vary property appreciation rates, rent appreciation rates, inflation, mortgage interest rates and the stock market rate of return?

It is important to realize that because the property prices vary with each run sometimes the properties they're buying can be slightly more or less expensive. On average though, property prices are going up at about 3% per year.

Rent is similar. Rents can go up or down, but overall, rents are increasing by about 3% per year.

Mortgage interest rates started at about 8.5% for a non-owner-occupant loan without paying significant points. But, mortgage interest rates can get better—or worse—over time as they're acquiring properties. That means sometimes properties will cash flow better and sometimes they'll cash flow a little worse.

Let's look at their journey to financial independence buying ten 20% down payment rentals in Error! Reference source not found..

You can see there are times when the market goes in their favor (both the real estate and stock market) they achieve financial independence early. And, there are times when they still don't quite achieve it through 60 years.

How does it compare to the two previous strategies: renting and investing exclusively in stocks and buying an owner-occupant property and exclusively investing in stocks? See Error! Reference source not found..

It is getting harder to see what is happening in the chart as we add additional comparisons.

We can make it easier in two different ways. First, we can look at the same chart, but turn off the shaded areas for each strategy.

This would leave just the median—or the middle-most result—where half of them are better and half are worse. That's Error! Reference source not found..

This chart doesn't show up the range of results (how early or late they achieve FI) but it does show how much more they're likely to earn by buying the rentals by what percent of their financial independence goal they're earning.

By earning a higher percentage of the amount they need to be financially independent, they're able to support a higher standard of living.

In other words, if they needed to be earning $10,000 per month passively to be considered financially independent, but their earning 200% of that—or $20,000 per month—they could live at a much higher standard of living on $20,000 per month than the $10,000 per month that they needed—at a minimum—to be considered financially independent.

The second way to make it easier to see what is happening is looking at the percentage of the 1,000 runs that achieved financial independence like we did previously. That's Error! Reference source not found..

Buying ten 20% down payment rentals sees them achieving financial independence earlier (more left on the chart above) and then has a similar success rate to what they'd see if they bought an owner-occupant and invested in stocks.

Owner-Occupant, Rentals and Stocks

I think you know what's coming next: what if they bought an owner-occupant property with 5% down, then bought up to nine more rental properties, each with 20% down payments and invested the rest in stocks?

With static assumptions that's about 3.5 years faster than just renting and buying ten 20% down payment rentals. See Error! Reference source not found..

If we do Monte Carlo modeling, it looks like Error! Reference source not found..

Doing a very busy version of this chart by comparing it to the other strategies so far, it looks like Error! Reference source not found..

If we just look at the 50th percentile (median) value for the four options as seen in Error! Reference source not found..

It shows that buying the owner-occupant property and nine 20% down payment rentals appears to be faster and gives them a higher standard of living than even buying ten 20% down payment rentals.

If we look at the percentage of the 1,000 runs for reach strategy that achieved financial independence and when, we can see that buying an owner-occupant property and then nine 20% down rentals is the best performer yet as seen in Error! Reference source not found..

In the chart above you can see that not only does financial independence tend to happen faster (a little to the left on the chart), it also tends to be more consistent (a higher percentage of the runs achieve FI).

Nomad™ Real Estate Investing Strategy Example

There's so much more we could do with this, but for now I'll wrap it up with a slight curve ball.

Instead of buying an owner-occupant property and then buying nine 20% down payment rentals, let's imagine they Nomad™.

- They buy an owner-occupant property with 5% down payment.
- They live there for *at least* a year. That's a requirement of the lender to get an owner-occupant loan with an owner-occupant down payment and owner-occupant mortgage interest rate.

- Once their year is up AND they've saved up enough for another 5% down payment, they buy another owner-occupant property and move into it.
- They take the previous property they were living in and convert it to a rental property
- They repeat this until they have 9 rentals and the property they're living in

Instead of having to save up for 20% down payments, they acquire the same nine rental properties with only 5% down on each by moving into each one as an owner-occupant.

Is this better? Is this more probable for them to be financially independent? Is this faster to financial independence? Does this give a higher standard of living than the other strategies so far? And—we won't cover it here because it is a longer discussion—but is it more or less risky?

It turns out that with static assumptions (not Monte Carlo modeling yet), Nomad™ is 58 months (almost 5 years) faster to financial independence. See Error! Reference source not found..

If we add variability and do Monte Carlo modeling, we can look at how the Nomad™ strategy performs in Error! Reference source not found..

Brace yourself for the busy version comparing them all at the same time in Error! Reference source not found..

And, if we turn off the range of results and just look at the middle most (median) of the 1,000 runs for each strategy, we can see the following in Error! Reference source not found..

Still a bit busy to see what is going on, but I will point out, in the chart above, the Nomad™ strategy seems to give them the fastest achievement of financial independence and highest standard of living.

Isn't it interesting.

If we look at the percentage of the 1,000 runs that achieve financial independence and by when you can see even better in Error! Reference source not found..

The Nomad™ strategy achieves financial independence earliest (to the left on the chart above). It also has a higher probability of being financially independent earlier.

Additional Modeling

Now that we know the importance of considering the variability that might occur in the future, this is really just the beginning.

There is a ridiculous amount more to dig into here. We've just barely scratched the surface.

There's a lot more to model.

For example, we could model each strategy you're considering seeing how each strategy performs:

- Buying long-term buy and hold rental properties (short-term rentals, medium-term rentals, student rentals, storage units, assisted living, apartments, etc)

- Buying properties utilizing creative financing (owner financing, wrap financing, loan assumptions, rent-to-owns, agreements for deed, subject-to)
- Variations on the Nomad™ strategy (Nomad™ by Proxy, Nomad™ with House Hacking, Nomad™ to Short-Term Rental, Nomad™ with Lease-Option Exits, *The Ultimate Real Estate Agent Retirement Plan ™*)
- House Hacking and related strategies
- Short-Term Rentals and related strategies
- Flipping properties and related strategies
- BRRRR and related strategies
- And much, much more

Or, combining one or more of these strategies at the same time (fix and flipping while acquiring long-term or short-term rentals as an example) or sequentially (fix and flipping for 10 years then switch to buy and hold).

Or, we could test a wide assortment of variations to your strategy:

- More or less reserves (and its impact on both speed and risk)
- More or less down payment size up to buying properties for all cash
- Buying down interest rates or not
- Getting roommates or not (house hacking)
- Selling via lease-options versus with a real estate agent or for sale by owner
- Paying off properties early with extra cash flow versus not

- Doing cash out refinances to buy additional properties faster
- Buying properties and selling them when you could take the proceeds (after all expenses including taxes) and then investing that money in stocks, bonds or something else to be financially independent
- Buying more properties than you need and selling them to pay off properties when it means you'd be financially independent
- And much, much more

Not Just Financial Independence

When we do these models, it is important to consider more than just how fast you're able to get to financial independence—even though that's what we focused on here.

Sometimes it is about your standard of living once you are financially independent. Some strategies might just barely get you to your minimum required income to be financially independent. While others will give you far more each month than you initially stated you needed allowing you to live at a much higher standard of living than you originally required.

Sometimes, it is about measuring, comparing and ultimately minimizing risks. Some strategies are riskier than others. They might get you to financial independence, on average, 1 year faster, but there's a 20 times greater chance you'll run out of money by pursuing that strategy than another one that gets you to financial independence, on average, a year slower.

That all might be worth considering... especially for your own unique situation.

It is important for you to evaluate your own strategy utilizing Monte Carlo modeling to better understand how to achieve financial independence faster, easier, with higher probability of success, with a higher standard of living and with less overall risk.

Or, if you are going to ignore one or more of those things, deliberately and strategically choosing to ignore them with full knowledge of the consequences.

212

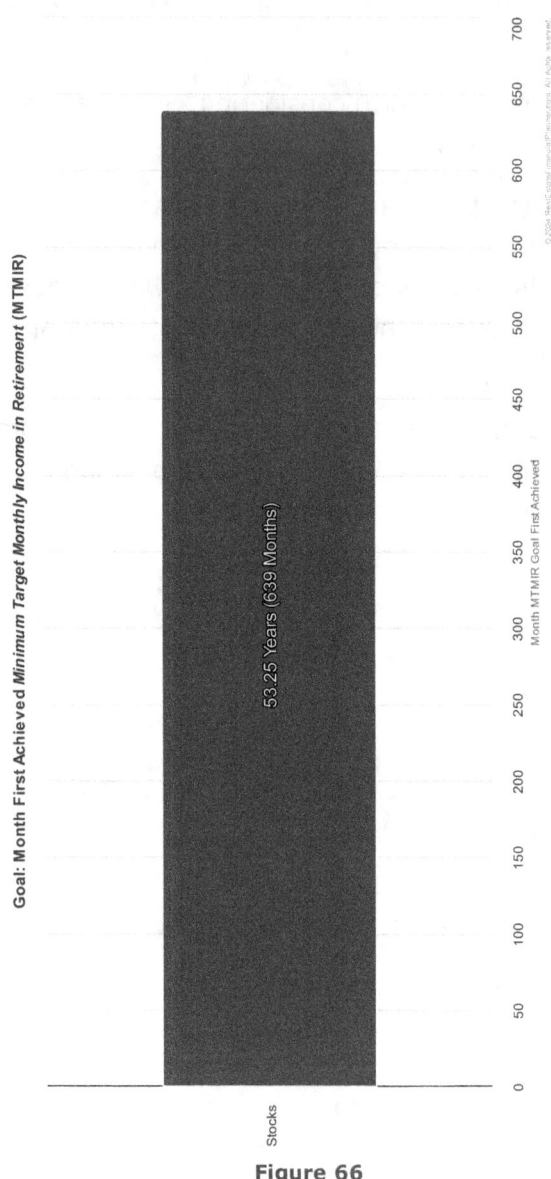

Figure 66

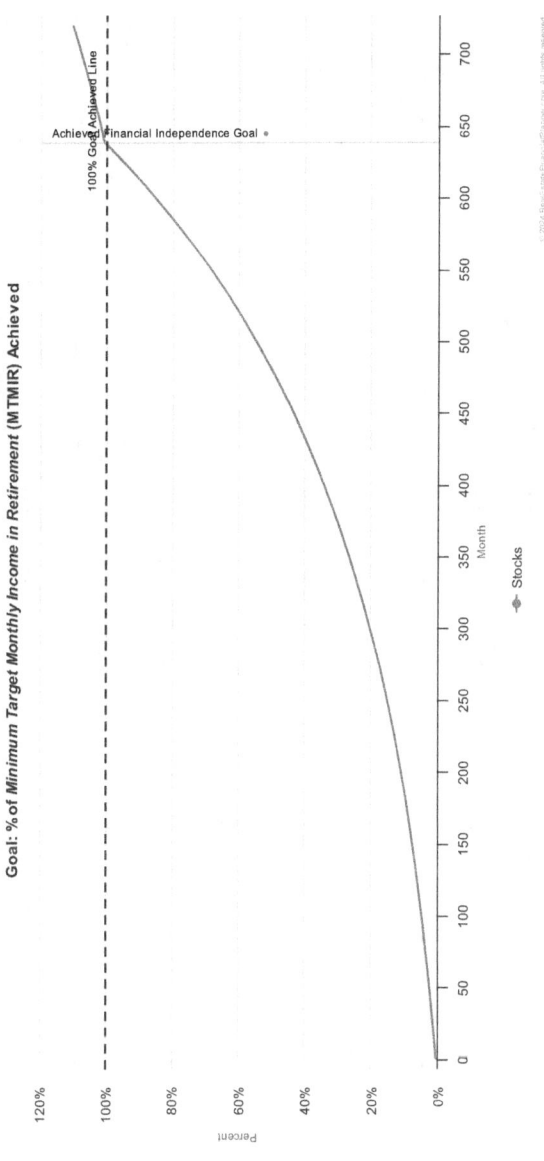

Figure 67

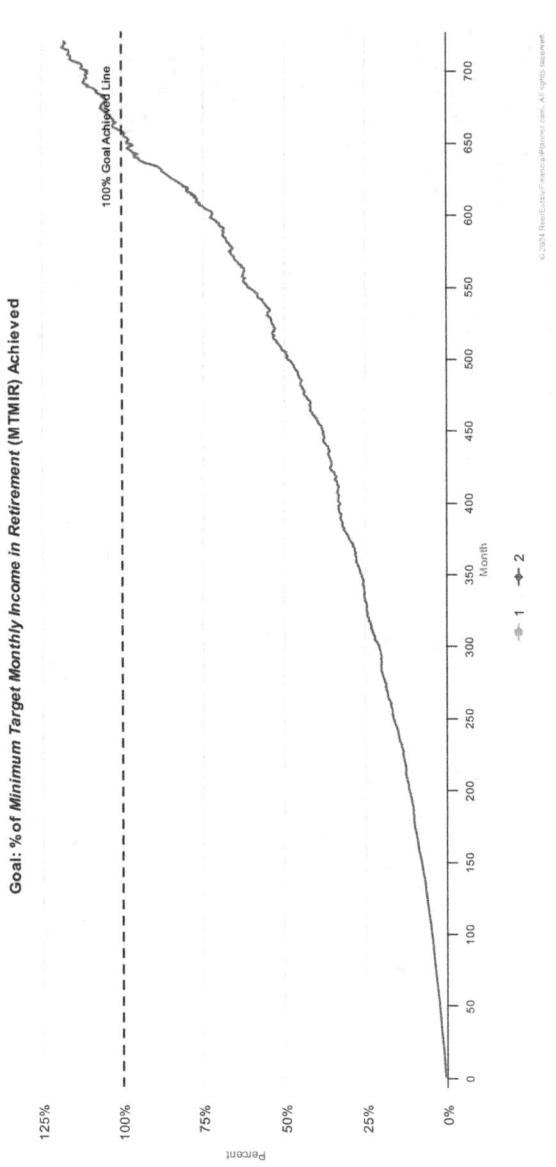

Figure 68

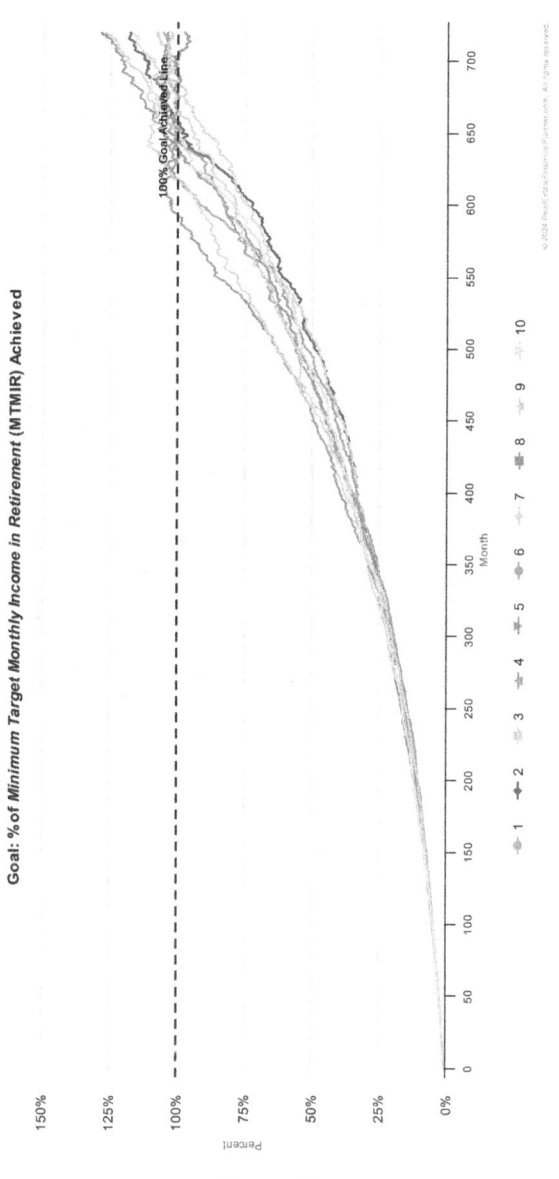

Figure 69

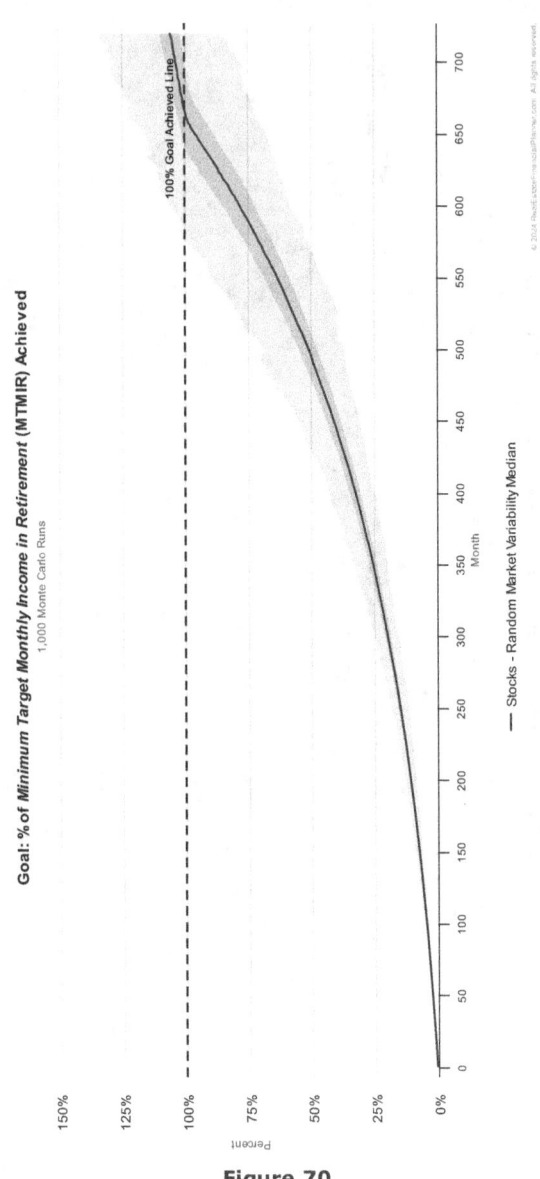

Figure 70

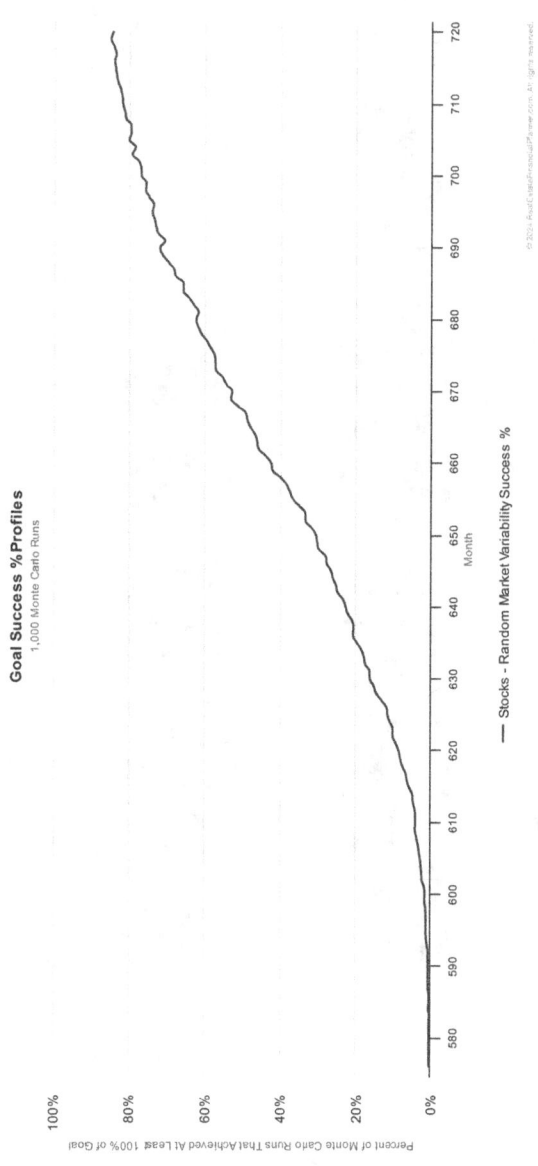

Figure 71

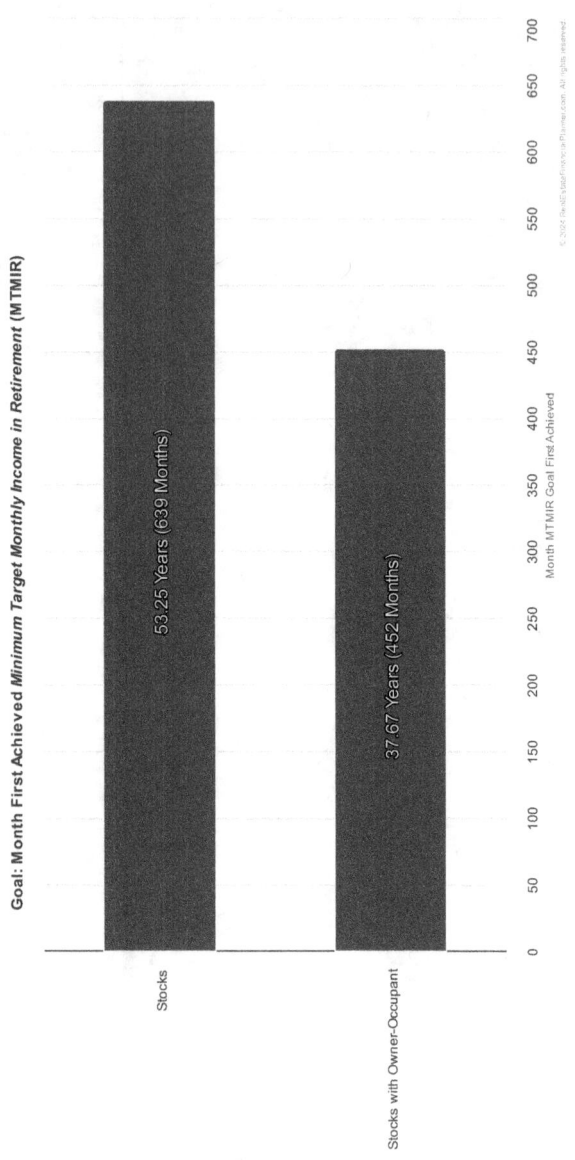

Figure 72

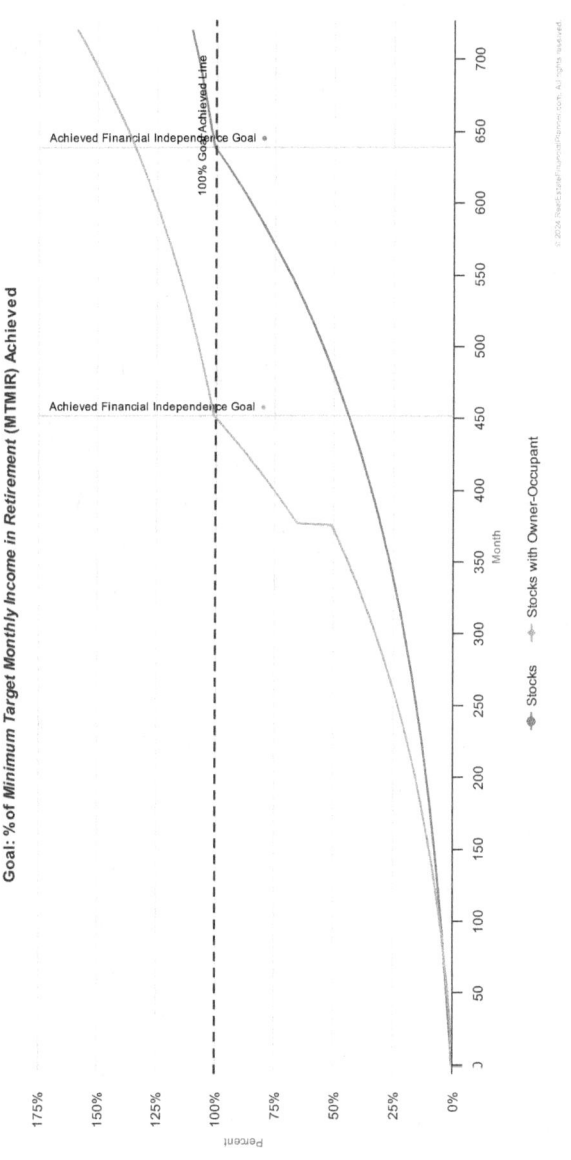

Figure 73

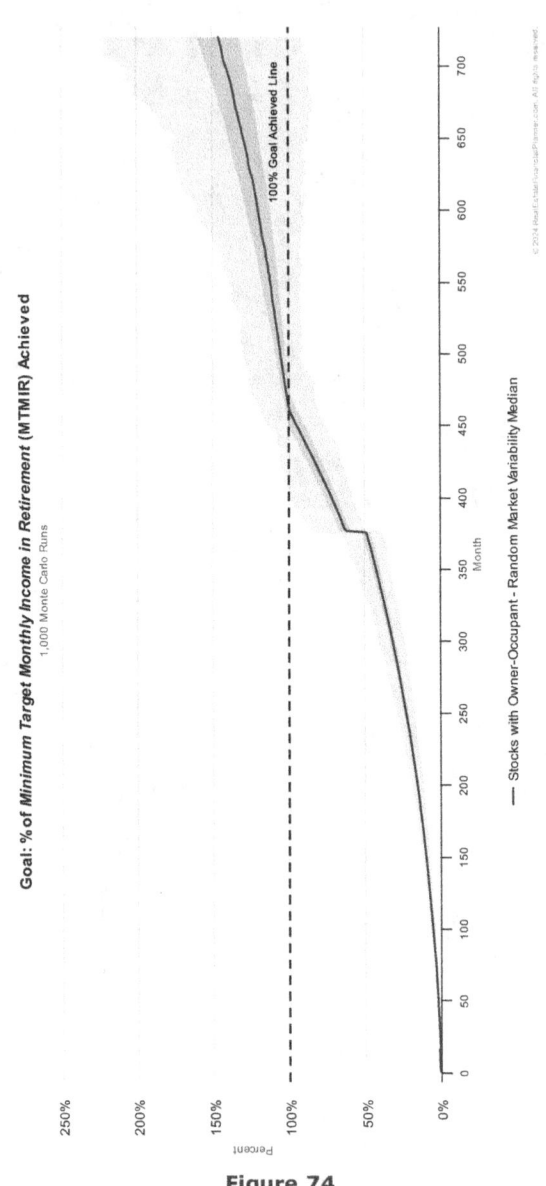

Goal: % of Minimum Target Monthly Income in Retirement (MTMIR) Achieved
1,000 Monte Carlo Runs

100% Goal Achieved Line

—— Stocks with Owner-Occupant - Random Market Variability Median

Figure 74

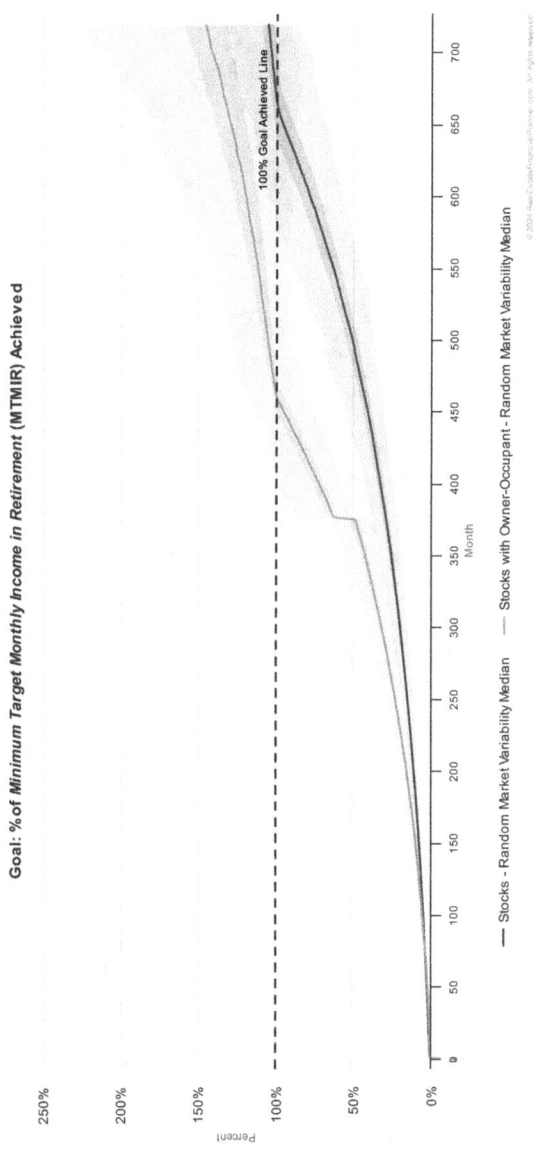

Figure 75

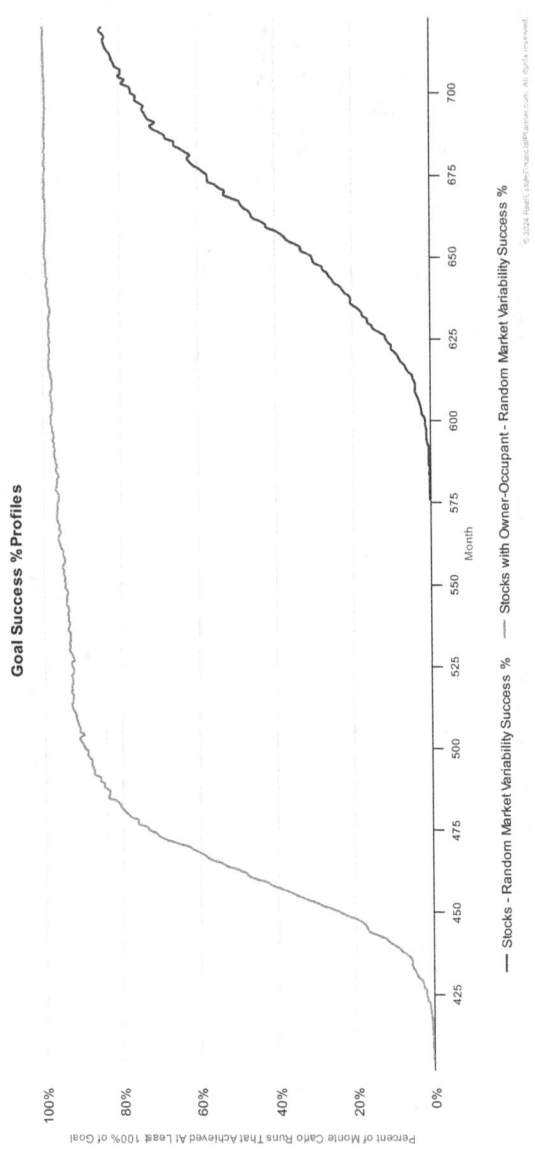

Figure 76

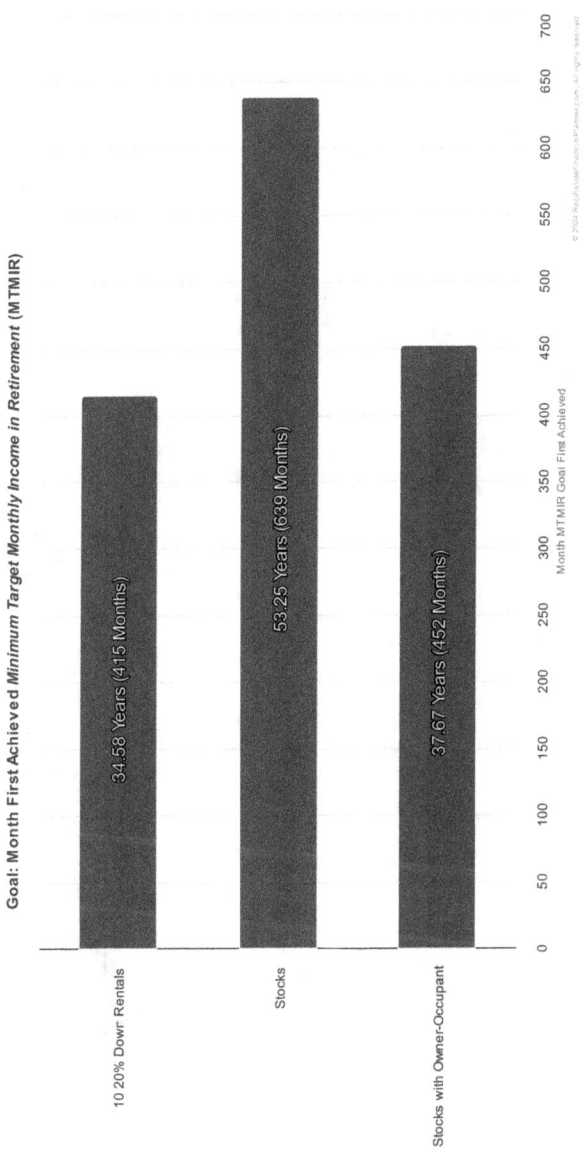

Figure 77

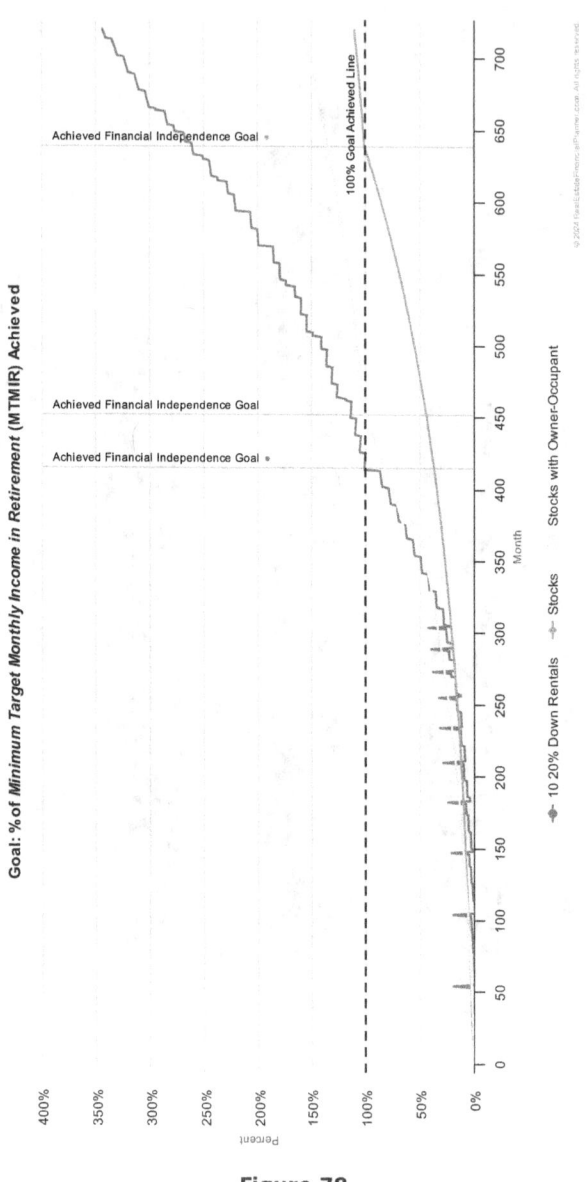

Figure 78

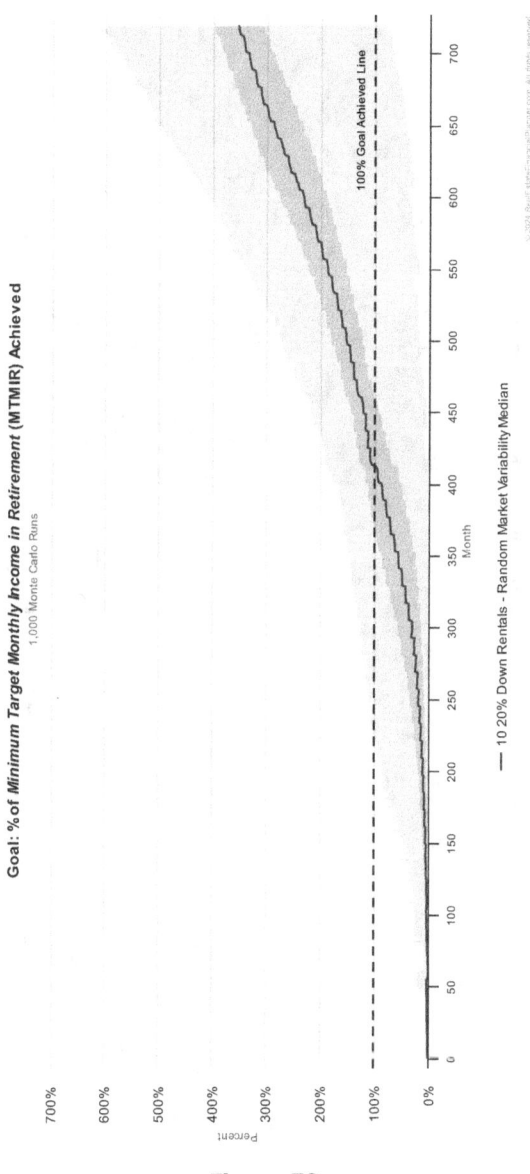

Figure 79

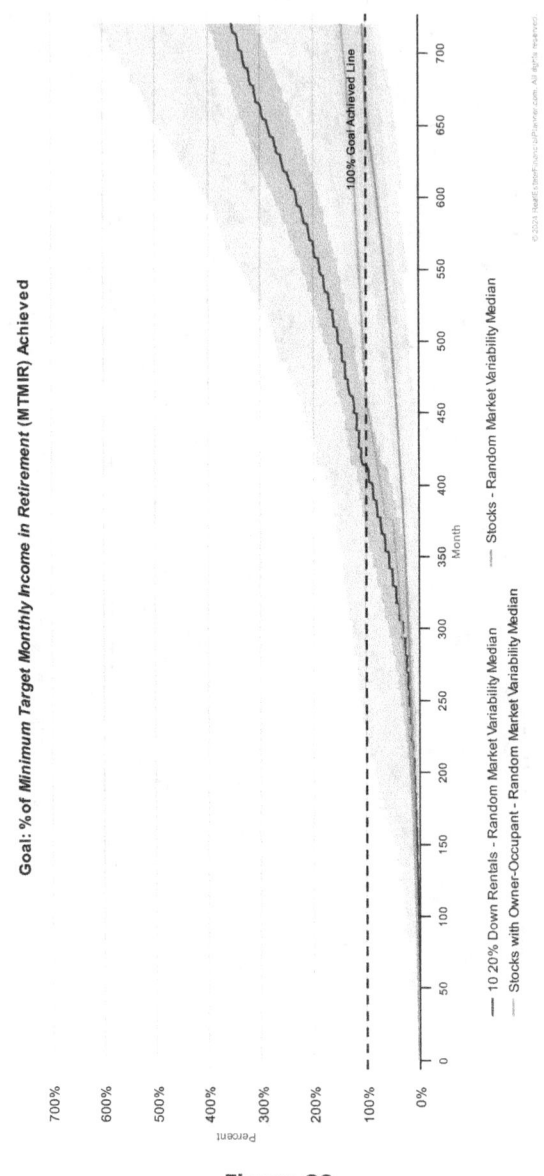

Figure 80

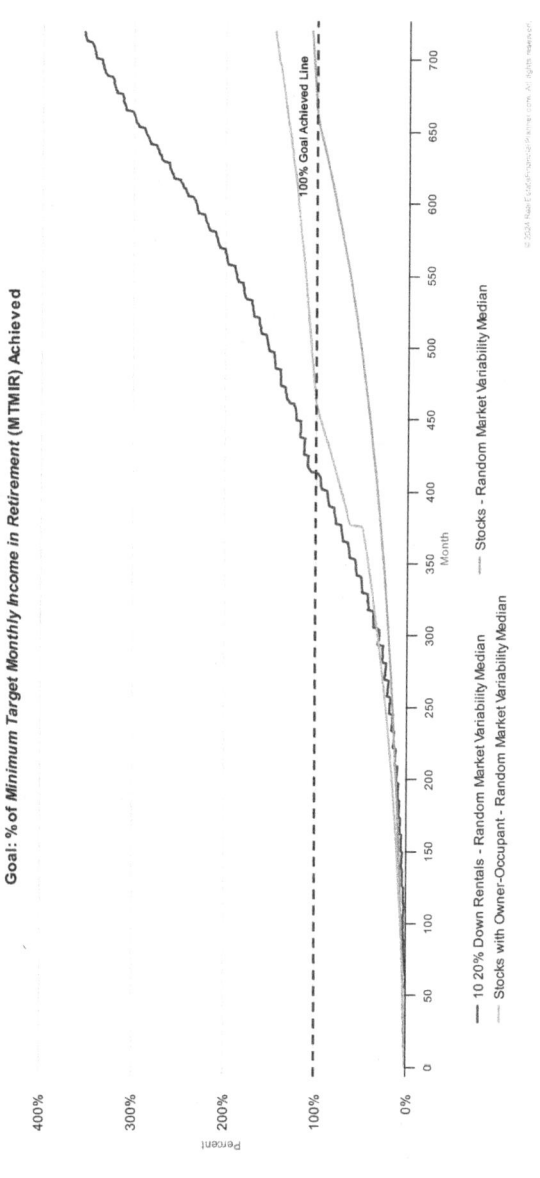

Goal: % of Minimum Target Monthly Income in Retirement (MTMIR) Achieved

Figure 81

228

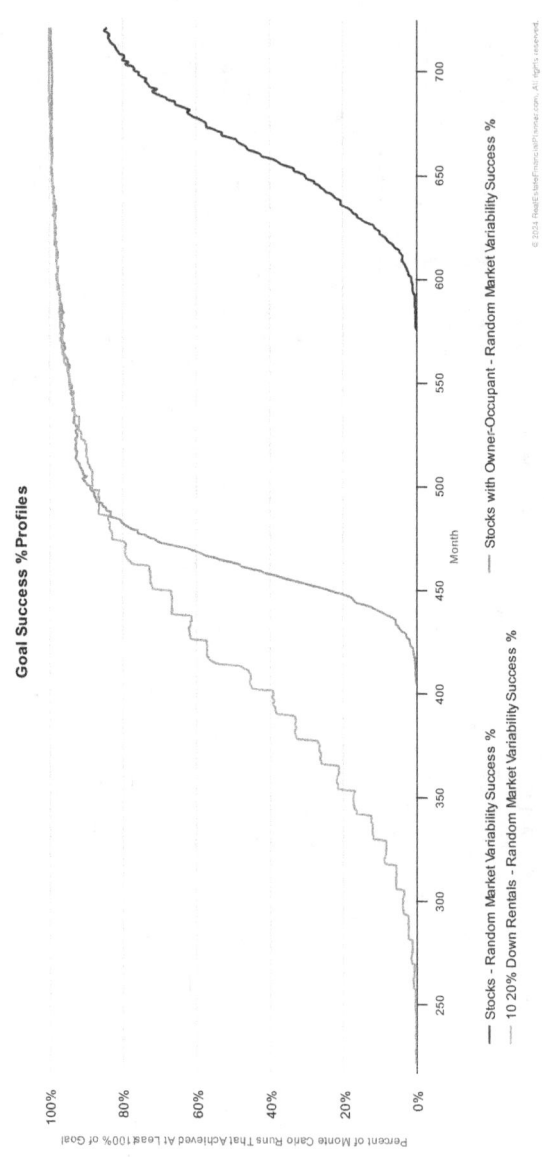

Figure 82

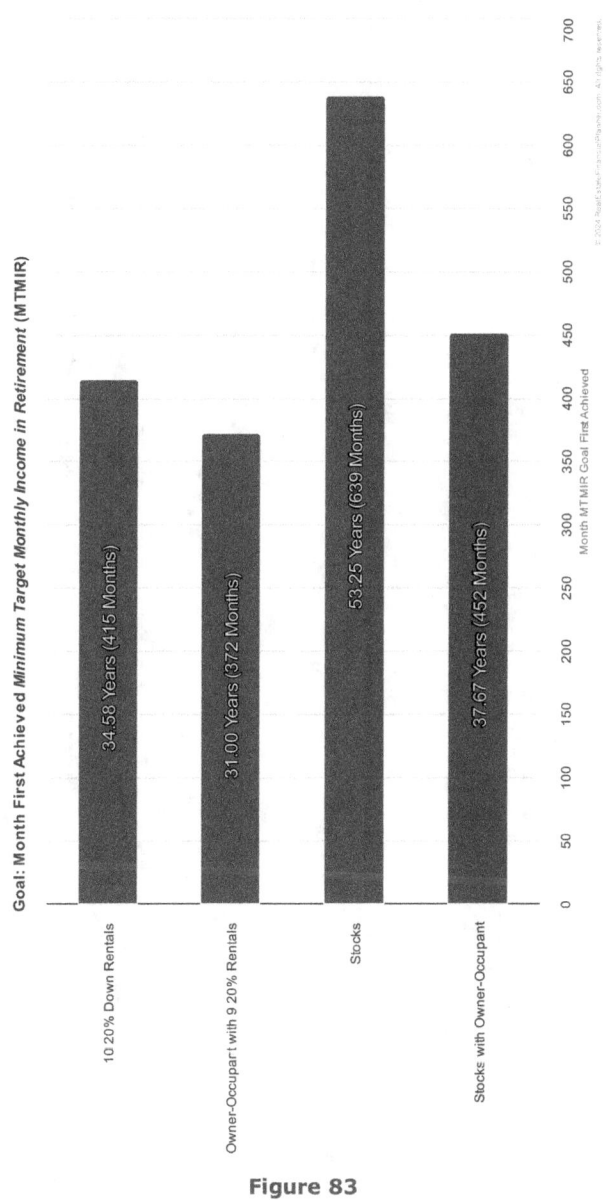

Figure 83

230

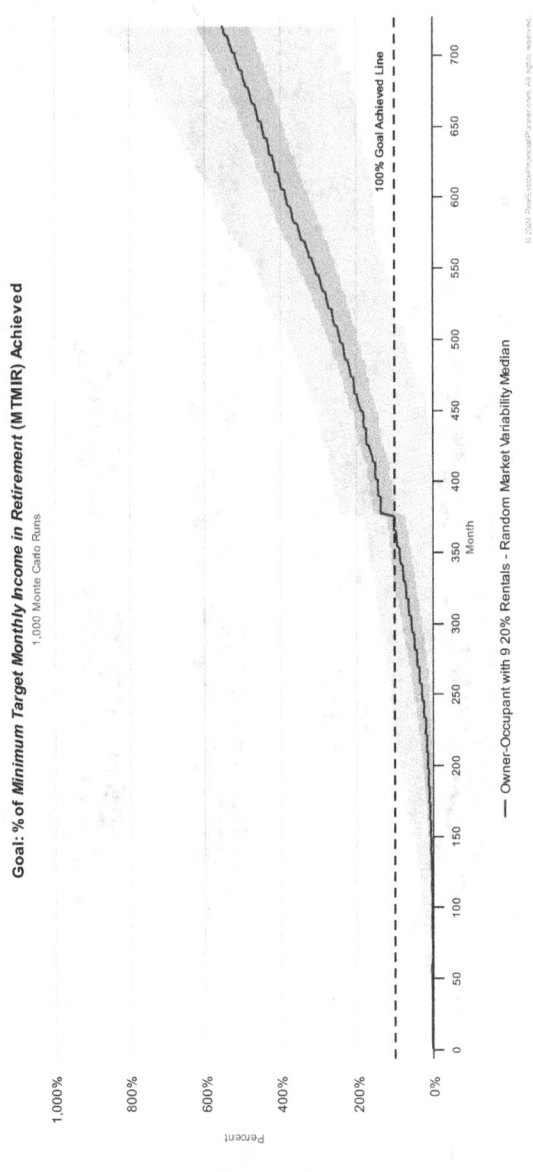

Figure 84

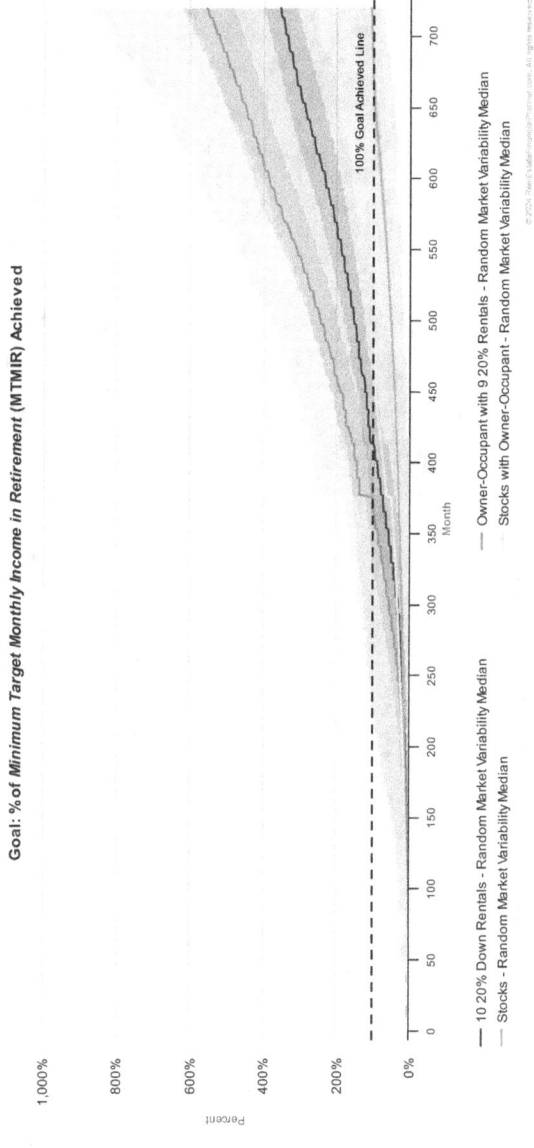

Figure 85

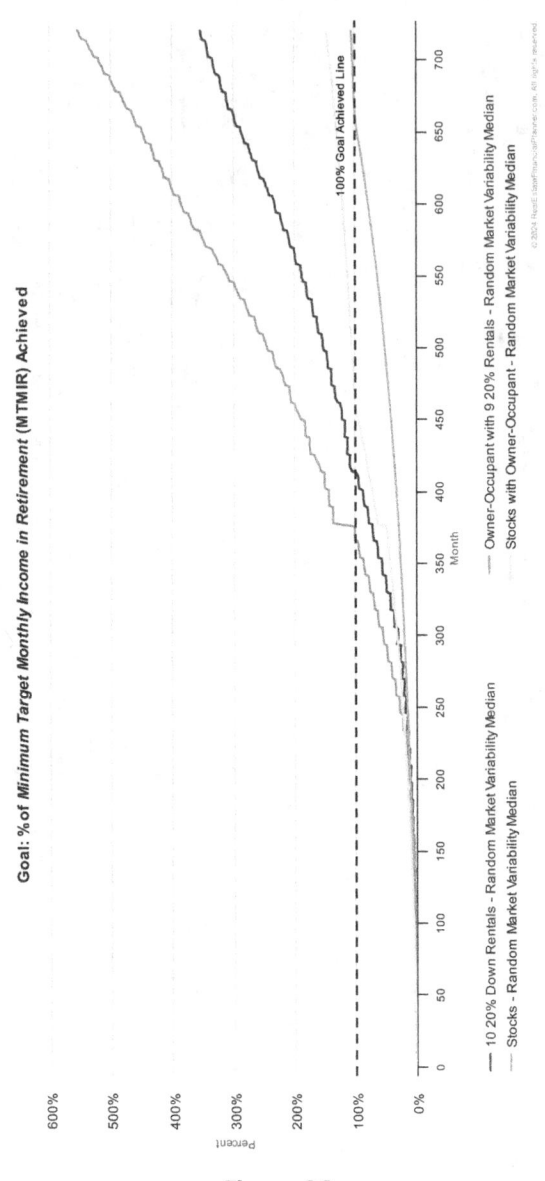

Figure 86

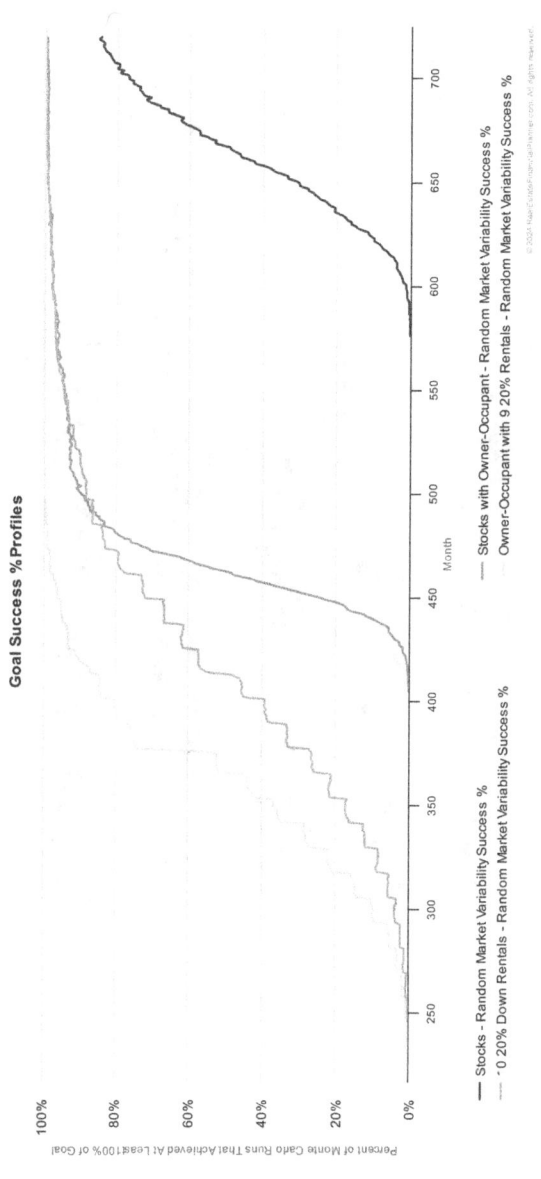

Figure 87

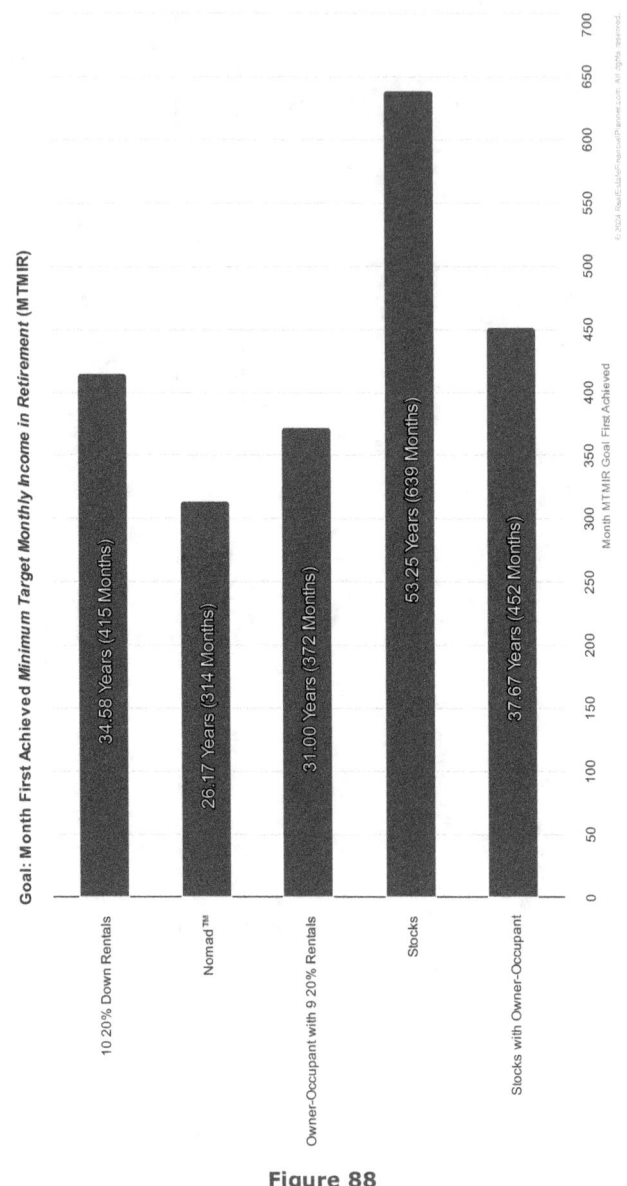

Figure 88

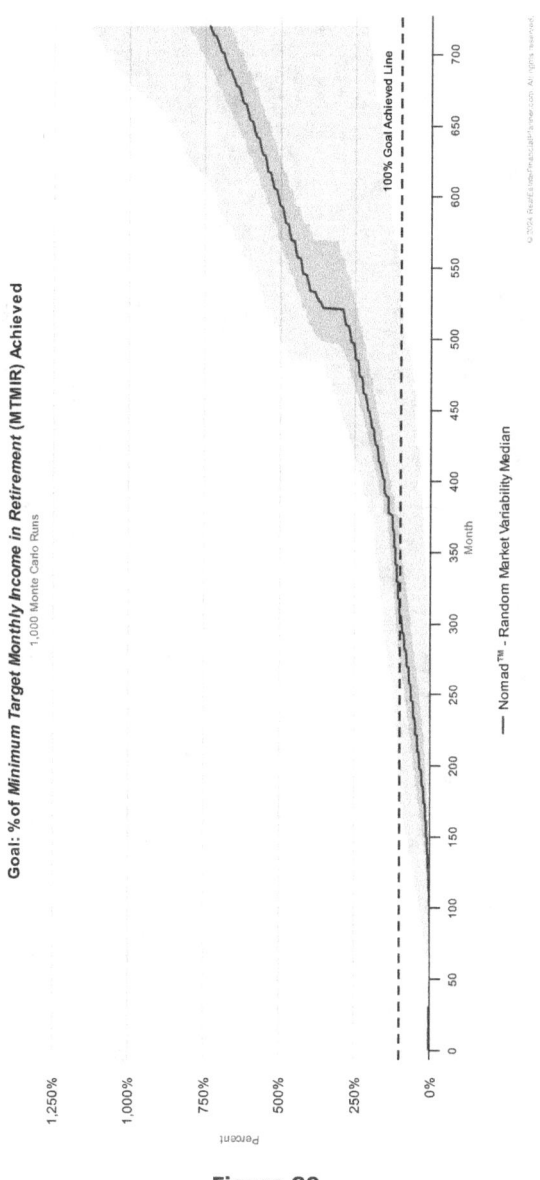

Figure 89

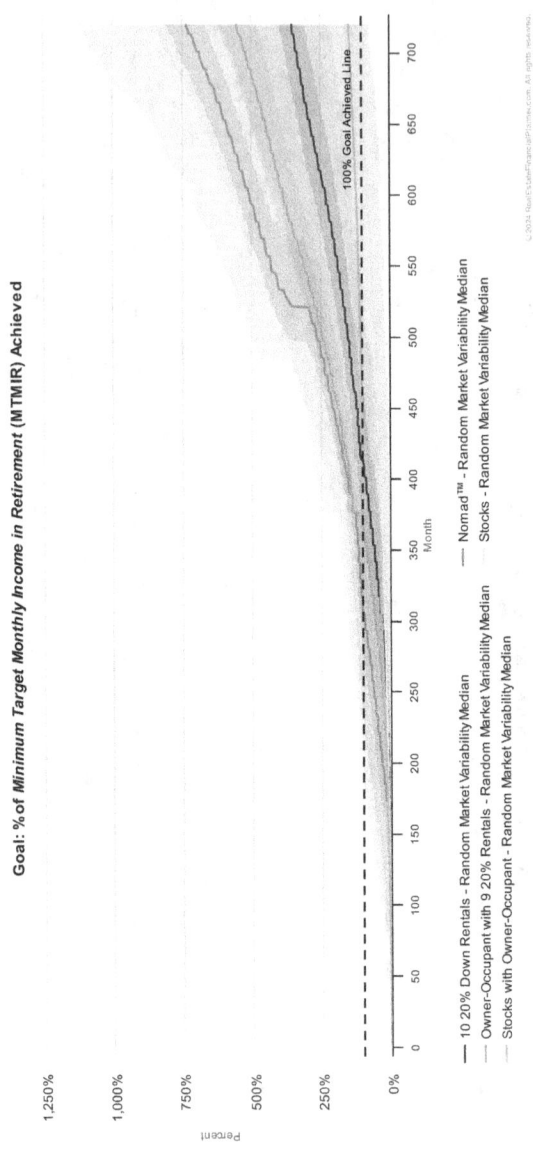

Figure 90

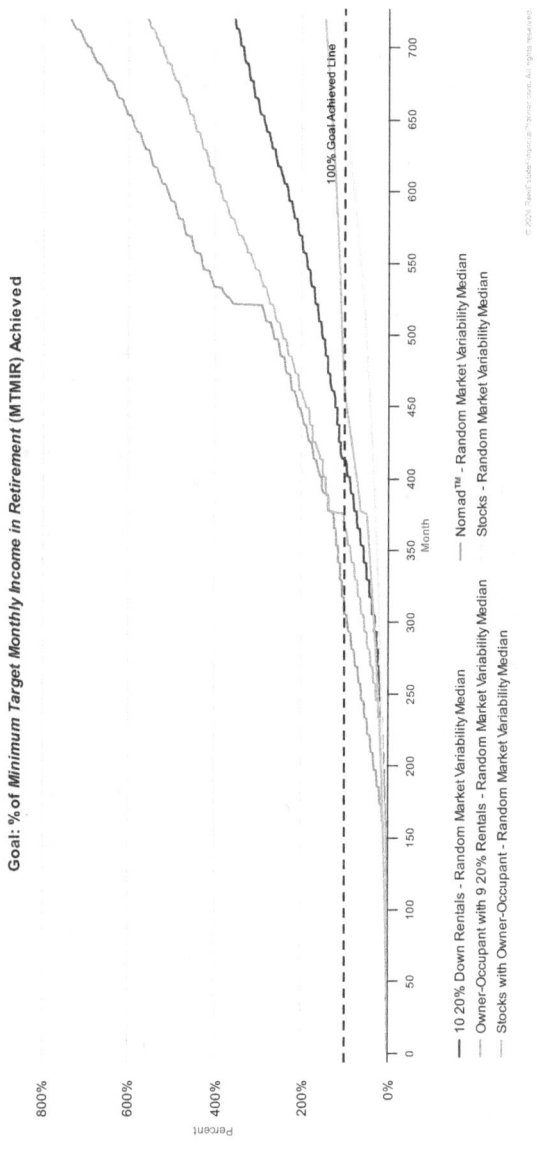

Goal: *% of Minimum Target Monthly Income in Retirement (MTMIR) Achieved*

Figure 91

238

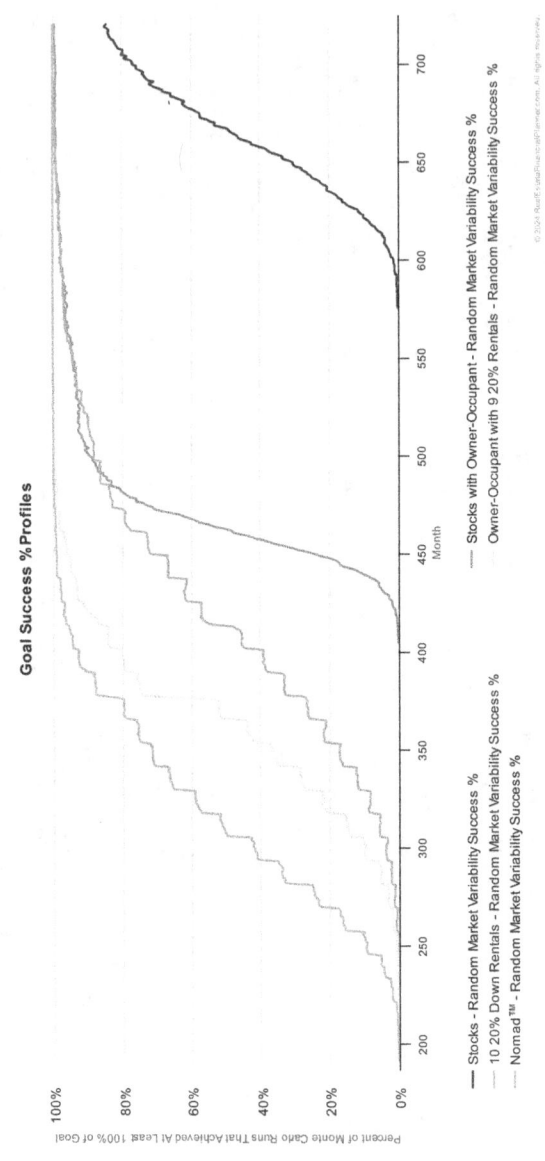

Figure 92

© 2024 James Orr. All rights reserved.

About the Author

James Orr is a seasoned real estate investor and the visionary creator of the Real Estate Financial Planner™ software. With a passion for sharing his wealth of knowledge, James has authored numerous books on real estate investing, covering a wide array of topics to help both novice and experienced investors succeed.

Living in Loveland, Colorado, James enjoys a fulfilling life with his wife, Tammy, whom he has been happily married to since 1995. Together, they have raised two grown sons. When he's not writing or managing his real estate investments, James is dedicated to teaching others the secrets of financial independence through smart property investments.

Also by James Orr

- The Real Estate Investing Mentor series of topic books
- How to Achieve Financial Independence and Live Your Passion Regardless of Age or Income: 10 Paths to Financial Independence Analyzed
- How to Acquire a Multi-Million Dollar Real Estate Portfolio With Just $3,000
- How to Acquire a Multi-Million Dollar Real Estate Portfolio Earning Just $5,000 Per Month
- Nomad™
- Ultimate Nomad™ Checklist
- Northern Colorado Real Estate Advisor
- Acquiring a Portfolio of Cash Flowing Properties In Northern Colorado: A Real Estate Financial Planner™ Blueprint
- Real Estate Investing Systems

Software and Spreadsheets

- Real Estate Financial Planner™ software
- The World's Greatest Real Estate Deal Analysis Spreadsheet™
- Should I Sell My Rental Property Spreadsheet™
- Should I Refinance My Rental Property Spreadsheet™
- CapEx Estimator for Rental Property – Basic and Advanced Spreadsheets
- Financial Independence Asset Allocation and Cash Flow Engines Spreadsheet™
- The Investor's Agent One-Page Business Plan™

A Small Request

Thank you for reading *The Real Estate Investing Mentor: The Affordable $50K Coaching Alternative* topic book on **Inflation for Real Estate Investors.**

I am positive if you follow what I've written, you will be on your way to successfully investing in real estate. When you do please reach out and share your story.

I have a small, quick favor to ask. Would you mind taking a minute or two and leaving an honest review for this book on Amazon?

Reviews are the BEST way to help others purchase this book and keep the price of my books low for everyone, and I check all my reviews looking for helpful feedback.

Please visit:

https://REFP.info/inflation-book

Questions?

Thank you for taking the time to read this book. If a concept sparked a question or if you feel there's an area that could be explained more clearly, I'd truly appreciate hearing from you. You can reach me at **jamesorr@gmail.com** with any feedback specific to this title. My goal is to make each book as helpful and practical as possible, and your input plays a big part in that.

Just a note—while I'm here to help deepen your understanding of this book's topics, this isn't intended as a personal coaching service. For advice tailored to your own situation, I encourage you to work closely with a real estate agent who can provide the insight and support unique to your goals.

Thank you again for reading, and for helping me make this series an even better resource for investors like you.